The
Trump's Politics Changed the

MAINSTREAM MEDIA DEMOCRATIC PARTY COMPLEX

and Why He Continues To Drive Them Mad

John Kinsellagh

Copyright © 2018 John Kinsellagh

All rights reserved.

ISBN: 9781728771120
ISBN-13:

Foreword	8
How it All Began	15
Trump Sets His Own Rules	17
The Media's Initial Trump Strategy	31
Press Corps: Hillary's Cheerleaders	43
Effect of Trump's Victory on the Media	57
Trump's Stunning Upset Was a Shock To the Media	59
Roots of the Media's Psychosis	68
No Honeymoon For Trump	76
Media Assault on the Trump Administration	89
Formation of the Resistance	91
The Russian Collusion Chimera	98
Media Merges Into the Resistance	109
Media Makes Themselves the News	115
A Malignant Presidency	128
FBI Spies on Trump Campaign and	

> Mainstream Media Yawns 138

Trump Returns Fire 149
> The Opposition Party 151
>
> Trump Abandons Media's Customs and Rules 156
>
> Trump Attacks the Media as Corrupt, Biased and Out of Touch 164
>
> The Media's enormous self-regard 172
>
> Trump Treats the Media With Disdain 178
>
> Trump Knocks Media Off Their High Horse 184
>
> Mainstream Media Digs Its Own Grave 192

Assault On Political Correctness 207
> Trump Assaults the Virus of Political Correctness 209

Irrelevance of Mainstream Media 221
> Media is Irredeemably Biased 223

Epilogue ... 226

Endnotes ... 230

Foreward

Over the years, the White House Correspondents' Association dinner has become for journalists, a gala of self-indulgence — a public forum for their collective virtue signaling and expressions of self-regard. At the 2011 dinner, then President Obama, mocked one well-known person in the ballroom by noting the man in question was exploring a run for the presidency. Much laughter ensued. Some say, at that moment, Donald Trump made the decision to throw his hat in the ring.

If Obama could have only foreseen the future, the revelation would have astonished him, as five years later, the object of his ridicule that evening, would be dismantling his "legacy" brick by brick. In a display of poetic justice, it would be Trump who had the last laugh that night.

Nine years later, all the beautiful people of the political/media establishment were once again gathered for the 2018 jovial affair. The only thing missing was the White House part of the White House Correspondents' dinner. The man who was the subject of Obama's quip at the 2011 event, was now president and decided, wisely, to skip the event — for the second year in a row.

President Trump's nonattendance at the 2018 dinner, didn't prevent members of the media, resplendent in their formal evening attire, from yukking it up among themselves in the ballroom, hobnobbing with Hollywood celebrities and other members of the jet set. The political journalists in the room were all self-absorbed, congratulating themselves as valiant watchdogs, holding a repressive president Trump at bay.

Members of the Mainstream Media-Democratic Party-Complex present in the room were political and cultural clones: all were unabashedly liberal; all were Obama progressives and all despised president Trump and fervently believed it was their sacred duty to help drive him from office at any cost. There wasn't an original thought or idea among them.

At prior occasions, Obama had previously been the object of the journalists humor and while there were some good-natured and pointed barbs, the White House correspondents dinners during the Obama Administration retained a modicum of decorum and restraint.

But the atmosphere for the vilify-Trump show in 2018 couldn't have been more different. The mood in the ballroom was combative and pugnacious. The individual who was supposed to be the object of good humor wasn't present. The dinner was a pathetic sham.

Michelle Wolf, the comedian chosen for the affair, took aim at the no-show president and instead of entertaining the audience with her wit, made the entire evening a tasteless orgy of Trump-bashing, all to the eager applause of a decadent audience of Washington journalists. Coarseness, masquerading as comedy, was the subject matter of her tirade. Those who were watching on television, must surely have been appalled at the crudeness of the purported jokes as well as the nastiness of the delivery. The spectacle was beyond the pale and indicative of an institution in the throes of irreversible decline.

The political media, with their tasteless and contemptible comedian of choice, may have viewed the event as a joyous and festive occasion for maligning a president they deplored, instead, it revealed to the nation their true selves; it bared their souls. All were willing members of the Resistance. They believed it their duty to speak truth to power and hold the menacing and malevolent president Trump accountable. They fancied themselves the guardians of our liberties, toiling valiantly on behalf of a grateful public. The theme of the evening was the First Amendment; the choice of a potty-mouthed B-grade comedian purportedly an example of free speech in action.

The only thing worse than the vulgarity displayed by Michelle Wolf, was the correspondents, reporters, anchors and pundits who all laughed, with reckless abandon, at the "jokes." Had they any sense of propriety or good sense, these elite members of the mainstream media should have voted with their feet.

For journalists, the 2018 correspondents dinner took place under a menacing cloud of profound transformation. The uncouth comedy of errors on display was a nervous reaction to a new political reality: the influence and power of the mainstream media under the new president began its process of terminal decline. Perhaps Obama himself presaged the beginning of the end for the mainstream media, when he said in jest to the journalists gathered at the 2011 event, "Most of you covered me. All of you voted for me."

The 2018 dinner was a signature event because it represented the nadir of the mainstream media's corruption, their enormous self-regard, overt bias and insularity from the public, on whose behalf they ostensibly labor. The uncultured attacks against president

Trump at that dinner brought to the fore the mainstream media at its absolute worst, indicative of an institution that had slowly and inexorably drifted into irrelevance.

By refusing to attend what had degenerated into a nauseating display of institutional narcissism, Trump sealed the fate of the White House Correspondent's dinner as well as the future of political journalism. His absence diminished the event, perhaps irreparably. Michelle Wolfe's performance had the beneficial effect of exposing the mainstream media as nothing more than a mouthpiece of the Democratic Party.

The final curtain on the media's 2018 get-Trump show would be prophetic, for it would mark the beginning of the end for the assembled audience of smug, arrogant, out of touch journalists, who, from that moment on, would further corrupt an already incorrigible institution with their fanatic zeal to drive the president from office.

For the media, the moment Trump announced his candidacy in June 2015, the battle lines were drawn. The struggle would continue and intensify once he was in office. But, as Washington media elites would quickly learn, much to their chagrin, Trump was unlike any other president or any other Republican journalists had encountered. More importantly, he refused to play by their rules.

After the momentous 2016 election, it would be the Mainstream Media-Democratic Party-Complex that ultimately would be vanquished by the new Sheriff in town. The stupor this unexpected and discomfiting reality induced within the ranks of the political media would end up driving them mad.

Part One
How it All Began

CHAPTER ONE
Trump Sets His Own Rules

Trump's unorthodox style and radical departure from established norms of political behavior, is one of the reasons that he was so singularly effective in offending the sensibilities of the media. When Trump burst on the scene in June, 2015, they were wholly unprepared for the show that awaited them from a man, who not only was a successful real estate developer, but who also was a consummate entertainer. Trump was not a politician, nor an attorney or a Washington insider: he was the consummate outsider, who had his own set of rules, his own way of speaking and his own unique way of dealing with the press.

Trump was not a product of Yale or Harvard and the social circles in which many of the political and media elites travelled, but rather, a product of Queens and the rough and tumble of the New York City commercial real estate business. He was brash, indelicate, and unschooled in the ways of Washington political-speak. As such, many in the chattering classes considered his unwillingness to conform to Beltway traditions a fatal character defect that would inevitably doom his candidacy. No one liked Trump's plain, forthright and wholly unscripted way of speaking and delivering his message except those who voted. One of the most important tell-tale, signs missed by political analysts and commentators during this election wast that after years of listening to glib, focus group tested, poll driven and insincere discourse from consultant-schooled politicians from both parties, Trump's supporters found his direct, unpretentious and unadorned method of speaking not only refreshing, but welcome.

Even though their expectations for Trump may have been low, reporters and commentators believed that he would not breach the etiquette and unwritten rules by which all candidates were bound. In this sense, the media was stunned by Trump because he was unlike any other Republican they had ever encountered. Trump made it very clear that he would not subscribe to the suffocating dictates of political correctness that had all but destroyed political discourse in the nation.

Trump correctly sensed what no other Republican candidate could and that was that many in the working classes who didn't live in the cosmopolitan urban enclaves were reluctant to air their true political and cultural beliefs for the not unwarranted fear that they would be stigmatize as racists, homophobes, etc. Instead of tempering his rhetoric, as many pundits had suggested, instead of staying within the permissible parameters of political discourse defined and enforced by the media, after his announcement, Trump continued to speak his mind and that of many others, when he assailed directly and forcefully the shibboleths of the Left.

When a Republican candidate makes a controversial statement, or more accurately, refuses to abide by or deviates from politically correct stands, reporters and commentators always ask the candidate to retract his statement. The second prong of this well-established tactic is to ask other Republicans candidates if they will criticize or condemn the statement made by the candidate. This song and dance never works out well for Republicans, yet they continue to play the media's game year in and year out.

Trump didn't play along with this ruse. Despite outrage from journalists and commentators over his comments that crime and drugs follow migrants coming across the border from Mexico, Trump stood his ground. in an interview with US Weekly magazine, on June 26, 2015, he refused to retract his earlier statement. "There is nothing to apologize for. Everything I said is correct. People are flowing through the borders and we have no idea who they are, where they're coming from. They're not only coming from Mexico, they're coming from all over South America and the world." When CNN host Jake Tapper noted that the Mexican government called Trump's comments prejudicial and absurd, Trump didn't try walk back his statement but instead responded, "Mexico has not treated us well. Mexico treats us as though we are stupid people, which of course our leaders are. I don't blame them. China's even worse."

He refused to temper his rhetoric on the campaign trail so that it would be more acceptable to his detractors in the media. What Trump did when he first entered the race was to shred the media playbook that had been employed for more than thirty years. Every Republican presidential candidate in recent memory always played along and always the results were predictable: it would work to the disadvantage of either the candidate or the party.

When fellow Republicans, in lockstep with commentators, criticized Trump for his indecorous remarks about illegal immigrants from Mexico, Trump merely shrugged it off. When Rubio called Trump's comments about Mexicans "offensive, inaccurate and divisive."what was Trump's response? After Mexican illegal immigrant Francisco Sanchez apparently killed 32-year-old Kathryn Steinle in San Francisco in a random attack Wednesday,

Trump sent a direct tweet to Rubio:"What do you say to the family of Kathryn Steinle in CA who was viciously killed b/c we can't secure our border? Stand up for US," Trump tweeted.

Shortly after entering the race, Trump immediately began attacking many sacred cows of the Left and the media with a vengeance. Commentators and reporters excoriated him for the infelicitous way he attacked, openly and without remorse, many of the sacrosanct tenets of liberalism.

Trump didn't care one whit what the media thought about him or his message. Journalists were stunned and angry that they were unable to moderate his behavior during the primaries.

Before Trump arrived on the political scene, the whole country was awash in a stifling swamp of political correctness run amok. The speech police were omnipresent and unforgiving to those who didn't conform to the catechism of progressivism in word and deed. Academic institutions birthed new theories and concepts to feed the diversity beast's need for instances of perpetual grievance. "White privilege" was the latest socioeconomic theory birthed on college campuses and implicitly incorporated into the Democratic Party's platform. Any criticism of the extremism expressed by the Black Lives Matters movement was verboten.

During the previous eight years, free speech was under assault. The Obama Administration seemed more interested in what bathrooms transvestites should be allowed to use rather than in the plight of the unemployed in the nation's great heartland. Curt Schilling, the famed Boston Red Sox pitcher and commentator for ESPN, was cashiered by that network for his alleged misconduct in having the audacity to suggest that men should use the men's room and vice versa.

Trump took the political correctness handbook, enforced by the media and assiduously followed by establishment Republicans, and he committed it to the flames. The act of defying the political communication rulebook immediately incurred the wrath of political journalists, who continued to labor under the illusion, that by holding Trump's feet to the fire for his indecorous and descriptive language, they could shame him into toeing the line and communicating according to the rules they had previously established for appropriate political discourse. They were badly mistaken.

Trump's frontal assault on political correctness was an enormous factor in securing his victories, both in the Republican primaries and ultimately, in the general election. Unlike the handsomely paid Republican consultants, who had overseen the disastrous two prior election contests, Trump was the only Republican who understood clearly at the beginning of the race that no matter what a Republican candidate said on the campaign trail, the media was always going to be hostile and critical when it came time to square off against the Democrat.

In this regard, Trump shredded the conventional wisdom of party elites and rewrote the playbook for Republican presidential candidates in terms of interacting with the media on the campaign trail.

During the primaries, the media was happy to play along with Trump's antics and give him free air time because doing so greatly enhanced their ratings. The networks saw this as a prudent and profitable strategy; they all knew that Trump didn't stand a chance of winning; he was going to lose and lose badly. There was no harm then, in humoring him during the primaries and ultimately, the general election contest against Hillary. They would make him look like a fool and fulfill their predestined role, as official communications organ for the Democratic Party, in facilitating Hillary's ascent to the presidency.

Unlike leaders in the Republican Party, Trump was shrewd enough to realize how tired people were of listening to the latest proclamations of progressives concerning certain speech they deemed offensive and certain behavior — however innocuous — they deemed "hateful." He had his finger on the pulse of Middle America and no one else did.

Trump had no respect for reporters who tried to shame him for his unforgivable sin of failing to adhere to the political terms of "liberal speak." Trump made it clear early on in the race, that he would not be cowed by the criticism of journalists for his failure to abide by the unwritten rules of conduct for presidential contestants. This drove reporters and commentators quite mad.

Trump deliciously sparred with one reporter in New Hampshire who didn't care for Trump's forthright manner of characterizing children born in this country to illegal immigrant parents as "anchor babies."

At a town hall event in New Hampshire during the primaries, one reporter challenged Trump on his repeated use of the term "anchor baby."

The reporter asked Trump if he is aware that the term is "offensive" and "hurtful."

"You mean it's not politically correct and yet everybody uses it? Ya know what? Give me a different term," he shot back.

The reporter suggested he modify his language and instead say "American-born children of undocumented immigrants."

"You want me to say that? No, I'll use the word anchor baby," Trump said, as the reporter tried to interject again.

❀ ❀ ❀

"Excuse me. I'll use the word anchor baby," he concluded before moving on to another question.

Despite their willingness to oblige the Trump show during the primaries, political journalists never anticipated the antipathy Trump showed for their expectations of decorum by which all Republican presidential candidates were to be bound.

Trump cast this implicit agreement to the wind. He openly chastised reporters on the campaign trail and attacked the cable TV networks who assailed him for deviating from norms of political correctness. He had Univision anchor Jorge Ramos physically removed from one of his press conferences for infraction of the rules for asking questions. Trump, most notably, was unforgiving in his criticism of CNN, which had now, through its openly biased coverage of the race, become the unofficial media cheerleaders for the Hillary Clinton campaign.

What many journalists referred to as Trump's "controversial statements," on the campaign trail, were nothing more than his refusal to engage in the fraudulent habit of speaking in euphemisms in order to describe unpleasant realities, that if characterized properly and without blandishments, might subject the media's preferred policy positions to heightened scrutiny by the public.

Trump was a novelty on the campaign trail because he called things exactly what they were and when his plain and accurate depictions clashed with journalists lexicon in support of their preferred narrative, he was castigated as "divisive" and controversial.

CHAPTER TWO
The Media's Initial Trump Strategy

The relationship between Trump and the media was not always one of unrelenting acrimony. The nature of their interaction evolved over time. Marked initially by curiosity, derision by reporters soon followed. Later, during the general election, outright hostility from the political media became the norm, and on election night, it reached its terminal phase, expressed through rancor and rage directed at the country's new president.

In order to gain an appreciation for the neuroses that plague the media currently, one must go back to the beginning, June 15, 2015, when Trump descended the escalator of the complex that bears his name and announced his candidacy. A close examination of the media's transformation subsequent to that event and throughout the campaign is necessary for a comprehensive understanding of its slow descent into madness.

Trump's announcement speech was slipshod, shoot from the hip, ad libbed. Though he did have policy issues to present, he did it his way, in an inelegant, rambling, indecorous manner. This speech would set the tone for the remainder of his candidacy. Trump's campaign statements would continue to be brash and forthright; he would not temper nor change his rhetoric to please the media gatekeepers.

The mainstream media fired its first shot across Trump's bow shortly after his entry into the race. The reaction was swift and unforgiving. The talking heads had a field day: Pundits and elites from both political parties responded with derision and disdain. He was mercilessly mocked on the cable TV shows and relegated to the sidelines as a showman and clown — perhaps good for the ratings due to the entertainment value, but certainly not a serious candidate.

Minutes after Trump finished with his speech, CNN commentator S. E. Cupp dismissed it as "a rambling mess of a speech...I was howling. Howling." On MSNBC, host Andrea Mitchell snootily asked the former Democratic Governor of Pennsylvania Ed Rendell: "Do you have any doubt that this is anything more than a carnival show?" The opinion of most other commentators, both liberal and conservative, were identical. Longtime GOP consultant Steve Schmidt admitted to "laughing out loud" while listening to clips of Trump's speech.[1]

At the start, no journalist took Trump seriously. Nonetheless, because of his high entertainment value, which was good for their ratings, reporters covered the Trump campaign constantly. In the end, Trump was going to get walloped by Jeb anyway. So why not have some fun along the way? And in the beginning, that's exactly what the smug media thought they were doing. The consensus thinking was let this clown make a fool of himself, we'll all have a good time in the process and in the end, have a good laugh at his expense when he goes down in flames well before the Republican convention in Cleveland.

Though it was an article of faith among journalists that Trump wouldn't last long on the campaign trail, since they were all captives of the conventional wisdom, there was one baffling phenomenon that escaped their attention. No matter what Trump said, no matter what Trump did, he seemed to be the Teflon man. Though his approval ratings might drop momentarily, they would always remain steady, within the 40% to 43% range. With all the forces arrayed against him, particularly the Republican establishment, no other candidate in history would've been able to achieve this feat except Trump.

In order for the media's "free air time" for ratings strategy to work as planned, Trump's campaign, at some point, would have to implode as expected. As the "he can't keep winning" mantra chanted by the pollsters became incessant during the Republican primaries, the carnival barker, much to the media's dismay, kept winning and winning and winning.

Despite Trump's surprise winning streak, towards the end of the Republican primary season, there was not yet panic in the ranks of the press corps because there was still time for his defeat. Every pollster and political analyst had proclaimed authoritatively, that Trump would ultimately fall prey to the political laws of gravity from which no politician was immune.

Accordingly, "No need to worry," was the operative phrase among the media mavens who comforted themselves that they could continue to oblige Trump with free air time, because, even though he was dispatching his Republican opponents, the GOP would never be crazy enough to let him capture the nomination and become the standard bearer for the party.

In the end, this self-assurance, much of it reinforced by Republican consultants, strategists as well as commentators from both sides of the aisle, was all for nought when he captured the prize in Cleveland and aimed his sights at Hillary.

The first time the media started to panic during the election was shortly after the Republican convention, when Trump started closing the polling gap with Hillary. The impudent Trump refused to stick to the script the media had assigned him and play his role as the entertaining buffoon.

When Hillary's once substantial lead started to shrink, the media responded with alacrity to the "All hands on deck!" battle cry. Although pollsters and experts alike still proclaimed the chances of Trump winning were about the same as a comet colliding with the earth, journalists were united in their belief that they must never allow him to derail Hillary's rendezvous with history as the First. Woman. President.

Once Trump became the Republican nominee, the Mainstream Media-Democratic Party-Complex turned from viewing Trump as a highly entertaining figure that greatly enhanced their ratings, to an existential threat to their candidate of choice. Going forward, the mainstream media would now function as Hillary's Praetorian Guard.

After the convention, the coverage of Trump became decidedly negative. He was characterized by Hillary as a racist, misogynist, Islamophobe, xenophobe and a nationalist. This was the core of the Clinton campaign general election strategy. The media, who act as the official communications organ of the Democratic Party, similarly described and stigmatized Trump, and when he gained ground on Hillary, they disparaged his supporters as well. To the pundits, Hillary's derisive remarks about Trump's supporters wasn't a description that occasioned any opprobrium, but rather, it was a charge that was unequivocally true to all but the most unenlightened minds. The

Democratic Party-Media Complex parroted her negative comments about Trump supporters endlessly.

As Trump started to close the gap with Hillary and the prospect of a President Trump was a distinct possibility, a new theory of press partiality emerged: "false equivalence." This is a concept favored by Left wing media, especially the BBC, who helped pioneer the "false equivalence" canard to justify its refusal to present opposing arguments to the global warming hysteria hoax. These acts of censorship are warranted in the eyes of the BBC and other progressives, because after all, "the science is settled."

After the election, Christine Amanpour used "false equivalence" to justify the new role of journalists as advocates and bulwarks against an oppressive and sinister Trump regime.

As Victor Davis Hanson noted, "During the 2016 campaign, James Rutenberg of the New York Times reminded journalists that they should feel no need to treat the exceptional

Trump candidacy by "normal standards," a de facto admission that journalistic crusaders would take the political lead in opposing Trump."

The false equivalence theory presumes, there are indisputable universal truths and these truths can be known only by liberals. In the case of Trump, the universal truth was that he was not a serious candidate, but rather a racist, misogynist, xenophobe, Islamophobe, etc., etc., and thus coverage of him should be openly biased and negative, given that he posed a mortal threat to the Republic.

Thus, late in the campaign, many journalists had no shame in wearing their partisanship on their sleeves. The prejudices of journalists was apparent and noticed by the public. In a prescient article, Justin Raimonda, writing in the *Los Angeles Times*, argued that the the Trump vs. the media battle was going to end very badly for the media. And the reason? Most people in the country were rooting for Trump: "Any objective observer of the news media's treatment of Trump can certainly conclude that reporters are taking a side in this election — and they don't have to be wearing a button that says "I'm with her" for this to be readily apparent. The irony is that the media's Trump bashing may wind up having the exact opposite of its intended effect."[2]

Raimondo further noted that,

> "Polls shows that journalism is one of the least respected professions in the country, and with Trump calling out media organizations for their bias, widespread slanted reporting is bound to reinforce this point — and to backfire. Trump's campaign is throwing down the gauntlet to the political class. If journalists are seen as the mouthpiece of that class, they may soon find themselves covering Trump's inauguration."[3]

Trump continued to shock the Mainstream Media-Democratic Party-Complex by throwing out the presidential election rulebook that had always been stacked against Republicans.

Late in the campaign, the media and Hillary were both dumfounded when Trump held a press conference before the start of the second debate and proceeded to introduce Kathleen Wiley, Juanita Broaddrick and Paula Jones, all women who had accused Bill Clinton of assaulting them in the past. The Mainstream Media-Democratic Party-Complex was apoplectic. Trump had broken the rules! He was a Republican! GOP candidates weren't allowed to fight back.

Trump's deft move was wholly unanticipated by journalists and network anchors and completely flummoxed the Clinton campaign. Trump's obliterating the War on Women narrative demonstrated once again, that he wasn't going to be bound by the rules established by the Mainstream Media-Democratic Party-Complex to which so many other Republicans had willingly subscribed.

Hillary's mainstream media enablers believed they could convey her "war against women" message with impunity by granting Bill Clinton an exemption for his licentious behavior. However, Trump forced the media to address Bill's philandering, his own well documented mistreatment of women, his dissolute behavior as well as the sexual harassment suit that was filed against him.

The media was infuriated, because the strategic plan for getting Hillary into the White House relied on a media code of Omertà with regard to the many instances of her husband's despicable behavior and depravity.

CHAPTER THREE
Press Corps: Hillary's Cheerleaders

Those who earnestly believe Trump is an enemy of a free press, would do well to review and digest the astounding partiality exhibited by the media during the election, including at times, outright collusion with the Clinton campaign. An unbiased analysis of the political media's Hillary cheerleading will demonstrate Trump was fully justified in treating the press corps with disdain when he assumed office because of the rampant bias and Get-Trump agenda of the mainstream media during the later stages of the election.

During the election, Hillary's Scooby Doo van was treated by a craven press corps as the

21st century equivalent of the royal carriage. Reporters, on cue, would chase down the vehicle and when Her Majesty emerged, they would hang on to her every word, which due to her ongoing email scandal, were sparse. Hillary peremptorily dismissed journalists, her lips sealed and they welcomed the abuse. Hillary treated her courtiers with appropriate disdain because she knew she was immune from any real probing questions or criticism because those who purportedly speak truth to power, in the end, were all rooting for the home team. The interaction of reporters with a haughty Hillary demonstrated the relationship was one of unrequited love.

Here is an example, as collected by Larry O' Connor, of some of the questions our intrepid reporters asked the woman who would be president after a 280 day absence with the press:

"You're on the cusp of being the first female nominee of a major party. What does that mean to you and how are you reflecting on that?"

"No matter what happens tomorrow, Bernie Sanders says the convention in Philadelphia will be contested. Do you think there is anything you can do to change that at this point?"

"Is it setting in that you might be making serious history tomorrow?"

"Some prominent Democrats have come out saying 'we maybe need to reevaluate the super delegate system more broadly. irrespective of what happens in this primary, do you support looking into that and, perhaps, getting rid of that?"

"Do you think Sen. Sanders will concede as you did in 2008?"

"What role would you like the president to play in your campaign?"

"Last night when you took stage in Sacramento, there was a woman standing next to me who was absolutely sobbing. And she said, you know, 'it's time, it's past time.' And you see the women, you see people here. People just come up to you and, {gasp} they get tears in their eyes. Do you feel… do you feel the weight of what this means to people?"

"Do you expect the president's endorsement some time this week?"[1]

Not one question about the criminal email investigation nor any inquiry about the pay-to-play influence peddling that occurred in the Clinton Foundation.

As *Investors Business Daily* reminds us, if left to the mainstream media, the story of Hillary's private server might never have been reported,

> "Normally, with a scandal this juicy and involving a would-be president, reporters would be falling over themselves to "advance the story." The reality however, was there always was a blackout on Democrat scandals. "But "normal" never seems to apply when a scandal involves a Democrat. The FBI has 147 investigators focused on the Clinton email case. One wonders how many investigative reporters the New York Times, the Post, and all the other big media outlets have."[2]

The groveling and obsequiousness that "reporters" displayed during the campaign was exceeded, if such a thing is possible, only by the hosannahs and praise heaped upon Obama during his campaign against McCain and later, when he occupied the Oval Office for eight years.

The mainstream media cheerleading squad for both elections remained the same, they just switched teams.

One of the reasons that Trump's victory against all odds was so significant is because his opponent wasn't just Hillary Clinton, it was the entire mainstream media, who from the start, were in her corner. In terms of Hillary's many advantages at the start of the general election, this perhaps was the most consequential, in light of her burgeoning email scandal and the media's willingness to protect her from the adverse ramifications of these bombshell revelations. Given that journalists had stacked the deck in Hillary's favor, one can understand how the political media would become unhinged when Trump defied the odds, surmounted the many advantages granted Clinton by the media, and beat her nonetheless.

At first the media's love affair was expressed by a blithe indifference to cover stories that would be harmful to the Clinton campaign, or by intentionally mischaracterizing her scandals as nothing more than the rumblings of the vast right-wing conspiracy. Later, when Donald Trump, whom the press treated as a novelty item or an entertaining circus clown, began to threaten Hillary's return journey to the White House, the policy of a virtual blackout on negative Hillary stories gave way to outright advocacy for the media's candidate of choice. The more Trump advanced on the inevitable candidate, the more overt the bias against him became. All pretenses of objectivity were jettisoned in order to respond to the clarion call to save the ship when the Clinton campaign began to crater.

Nowhere was this unabashed partiality by mainstream media journalists more apparent than in CNN's repeated refusal to discuss Bill

Clinton's mistreatment of women. Since it would be difficult to discuss Bill's aberrant behavior without looking at Hillary's indispensable role as his enabler, it was not surprising, that CNN news anchors would make it a habit to remind guests on the program who were Trump supporters, that the topic of Bill's well chronicled mistreatment, philandering and abusive treatment of women, was verboten —especially during the election, when the CNN host's preferred candidate, was running for president.

A perfect example was CNN anchor, Brooke Baldwin, who repeatedly shut down guests who brought up Bill Clinton's despicable past behavior. Here is Baldwin in one of her "see no evil, speak no evil, hear no evil" moments. When a guest started to speak about Bill's womanizing, Baldwin immediately interrupted her and stated that, "We're not going to air Bill Clinton's dirty laundry on this show."

Of course, Baldwin's blackout on Bill's past behavior came to an unexpected and ignominious end, when Trump held a press conference before the start of the second debate and proceeded to introduce Kathleen Wiley, Juanita Broaddrick and Paula Jones, all women who had accused Bill Clinton of assaulting them in the past.

Trump was especially loathed by journalists because for the first time, he forced the Democratic Party media to acknowledge and discuss Bill Clinton's well-known transgressions as a relevant topic during the election.

When listening to the media whine and complain currently about how president Trump is bashing the press, journalists need a reminder about the servile manner in which alleged "reporters" covered the Clinton campaign. A few examples will suffice. For starters, let's focus on the *New York Times* star reporter, Amy Chozick, the type of journalist Ben Rhodes, Obama's national security communications director, would have characterized as a 25 year old know-nothing. Chozick, who was on Hillary's speed dial, was the go-to gal for the

Clinton campaign. A common expression in the campaign office in Brooklyn when Hillary had suffered some adverse publicity, was, "Get Amy on the phone!"

An obsequious Hillary for President groupie, how Chozick could have ever been construed by her employer, the *New York Times* as well as the public at large, as a "reporter" is an endearing mystery. Chozick herself, thoroughly validates this observation in her tell-all book, *Chasing Hillary*, published well after the election, Chozick reveals candidly, that she was an unabashed Hillary booster since her pre-teen days, well before she was a reporter. When assigned to cover the campaign, her adoration did not abate.

The Wikileaks emails revealed the scope of journalists brazen and shameless collusion with the Clinton campaign in order to defeat Trump.

Glenn Thrush, a media paragon of "objective" reporting, sought prior approval from the Clinton campaign before publishing his stories. Naturally, the *New York Times* rewarded him for his impartiality with an offer of employment .

Dana Milbank, of *The Washington Post*, is another example of a Democratic Party yes-man. He contacted the Clinton campaign for opposition research he could use for an article on Trump, prior to publication.

Other Hillary boot-lickers abounded among members of the mainstream media. The list is a long one and presents a stinging indictment of U.S. journalism as nothing more than a tool of the Democratic Party. Anyone who questions this proposition in light of the overwhelming and unassailable evidence supplied by the interaction of journalists and the Clinton campaign is either shamelessly dishonest or has been residing on another planet.

The brazen partiality of the press, coordinating with the Clinton campaign, provides context with which to evaluate the legitimacy of the criticism that Trump was assaulting a "free" press and undermining journalists ability and sacred duty to inform and report the news to the public in an objective and impartial manner.

An additional reason for the media'a hands-off approach for reporting on Hillary's duplicity and chicanery was due to the gender element inherent in the catechism of political correctness by which all journalists were bound.

Indeed, so enamored was the press with politically correct reporting, that it severely impaired their judgment during the election, causing them to miss one of the most significant political events in recent history. Unsurprisingly, during the election, the mainstream media's reporting on Hillary followed its exact template for reporting on Obama: minimize, or omit entirely, negative stories that may be damaging to their candidate of choice. A prominent example? For most journalists, Hillary's email chicanery was a "nothing burger."

Reporters did not want to be accused of being anti-black or anti-woman. According to the gospel of identity politics, Hillary and

Obama were both members of a protected class and would be treated as such by the media.

In a rare moment of candor after the election, NBC's Chuck Todd admitted the media's reporting on Hillary was circumscribed by the dictates of political correctness.

In Todd's own words,

"And I think it was a fear of, 'Oh, is it going to look like it's sexist, anti-woman if we say that?'" he added, pointing out that on the hustings he saw numerous "Hillary for Prison" signs adorning the front yards of rural America. "I think we underplayed it a little bit out of political correctness fears," Mr. Todd said. "No member of the press corps wants to look like they're singling out a group and making a group feel bad, right, whatever that [group] is.

Todd all but admitted the coverage was definitively skewed because mainstream media journalists are not permitted to deviate from the catechism of identity politics, "Where I think political correctness got in the way of what we all knew as reporters and didn't fully deliver was how hated the Clintons were in the heartland."

   But, Todd implicitly seemed to believe that in all other respects, the media remained "objective." That is utter nonsense. The media is the personification of political correctness; it gives it life and succor. Since the media is now beholden or incorporates the pseudo-intellectual balderdash taught on college campuses subsumed under the rubric of "diversity", the only group that is fair game in this world of grievance- mongering is White Men. And, that is precisely why the media upbraided Trump's supporters endlessly, because they were not members of a cherished "protected class."

Part Two
Effect of Trump's Victory on the Media

CHAPTER FOUR

Trump's Stunning Upset Was a Shock To the Media

You could tell by their faces.

One by one, as key states were called for Trump during the night and the electoral votes tallied inexorably in his favor, the faces of the anchors, commentators and reporters turned ashen, drawn. Shellshocked, they gazed into the camera. When they spoke, there was disbelief in their plaintive voices. Some, spoke in hushed, somber tones, as if they had just been notified that a close family member had died.

There would be no coronation gala at the Javits Center, the planned festivities, now unceremoniously cancelled. Even though the fireworks crew had been pre-paid, there would now be no multi-colored light display over the Hudson.

Indeed, for many in the media, the atmosphere was appropriately funereal. The moment Trump approached the podium for his acceptance speech, came the painful realization, that their hopes, like hers, had been crushed.

The body language and reaction of the cable TV anchors on election night gave away the game in terms of who was rooting for whom. The reporters were all visibly weary from covering a contest that every pundit, commentator and cable TV anchor thought was a foregone conclusion. No matter how some tried, it was impossible to hide their sense of foreboding. Over at ABC News, reporter Martha Raddatz, who had clashed needlessly with Trump at the second presidential debate, began to cry.

Throughout the evening, the incipient resentment of political journalists and TV anchors, for the moment was suppressed, supplanted later by the horror and disbelief that the next president of the United States would be a reality TV star instead of the smartest woman in the world.

Election night despair, would be the catalyst for a collective psychosis that would soon grip the Mainstream Media-Democratic Party-Complex, finding its expression in unprecedented animosity towards a sitting president, in a manner not seen before in American political history. Even the vilification by the press corps to which Richard Nixon was subjected, was mild by comparison with the adversarial and acerbic relationship that ensued immediately for president-elect Trump.

Before the night was over, the explanations from many of these "expert" commentators began to trickle in: with nary a mention of Hillary's serial lies about her private clandestine email server, came the pronouncements spoken with certitude: Hillary lost, obviously, due to rampant misogny, among the bitter clingers; others blamed a dangerous emergence of white nationalism. Hillary's loss was a "whitelash" cried an unhinged Van Jones on CNN. This convoluted theory contends that even though Hillary wasn't an African American, the only explanation for her loss was that some of the same voters who voted for Obama twice, were now casting their ballots against the nations's first African-American president.

As soon as Hillary lost, Trump instantly became the object of liberals and the media's fury because he had bent the arc of history in a direction that identity politics progressives did not anticipate nor approve.

The ferocity of the criticism from media pundits and commentators was truly unprecedented. Writing in Fox News shortly after the election, Howard Kurtz noted, "When Hillary and her staff experienced shock and mourning the media followed suit. The first woman president now dashed, their dreams were theirs as well."[1]

Kurtz lists some of the unhinged commentary: "Jamelle Bouie, an African-American and a top political writer for Slate, tweeted: 'I didn't quite understand how much white people hated us, or could at least live with that hate. Now I do."

That was before Bouie apologized for misunderstanding the election but after he wrote that Trump "all but cried [the N-word]."

Not to be outdone, "Jeff Jarvis, a liberal media critic, author and blogger who directs a journalism program at the City University of New York, blamed the press, tweeting:

"I fear that journalism is irredeemably broken, a failure. My profession failed to inform the public about the fascist they are electing."

Jarvis also wrote: "I'll say it: This is the victory of the uneducated and uninformed." (He blamed others as well, including his race for "inherent racism," his gender for "sexism" and himself.)"

Jarvis' comments about Trump voters would be uniformly adopted by political journalists, commentators and cable TV hosts. Of course, since the president was now going to be Trump instead of Hillary, Jarvis's outbursts were understood as a normal and therapeutic response attendant upon "grieving."

In normal times, Jarvis' demented expostulations would insure his dismissal and prompt some soul searching as to how this progressive ideologue ever was appointed a professor of "journalism." Instead, Jarvis' outbursts would tellingly presage the course journalism would follow after the election.

If Jarvis could only see beyond his nose, he might have been able to discern, that the sniveling sense of superiority projected by his fellow travelers in the Mainstream Media-Democratic Party-Complex was one of the reasons that Donald Trump was in the White House.

The *New Yorker*'s reliable Trump nemesis, David Remick, writing in what is now nothing more than a communications subsidiary of the Democratic Party, erupted in progressive righteous fury,

"The election of Donald Trump to the Presidency is nothing less than a tragedy for the American republic, a tragedy for the Constitution, and a triumph for the forces, at home and abroad, of nativism, authoritarianism, misogyny, and racism. Trump's shocking victory, his ascension to the Presidency, is a sickening event in the history of the United States and liberal democracy."[2]

Some hard left CNN reporters and guest commentators firmly believed that Trump's win would signal the beginning of a wave of white nationalism, replete with a revival of the Ku Klux Klan that would squash minority rights; Muslims would now have to fear for their lives. One would hope that such hyperbole was purely the result of an outpouring of grief after Hillary's loss, but the journalists who made the comments fervently believed them to be true.

Here is an ominous sounding Leonard Pitts Jr. of the *Miami Herald*, intimating the parallels in Trump's victory to the rise of the national socialists in late 1930's Germany,

"No, it's not slavery, nor is it Holocaust. But it is something. That much, we can no longer doubt.

"And I am reminded of German Jews who watched a monumental evil gather itself against them, all the while assuring one another that things weren't as bad as they seemed, that their country would soon return to its senses. Meantime, the boxcars were lining up.

"To recall their response to a world suddenly grown ominous and strange is to wonder at our own. Maybe we are too alarmist.

"Or maybe we're not alarmist enough.[3]"

Following in lockstep, Vox pronounced that, "Trump's win is a reminder of the incredible, unbeatable power of racism."[4]

Members of the Mainstream Media-Democratic Party-Complex initially reacted to Trump's victory much in the same way as someone who has been unexpectedly punched in the stomach: shock, followed by a temporary loss of breath, disorientation, dizziness followed by a gradual return to equilibrium, which for the political media, now meant righteous indignation.

Because the shock of Hillary's loss, was a stunning blow to journalists they could neither process nor fathom, a post-election narrative was needed in order to assuage the widespread despair. Trump's victory was a fluke and had to be the result of some nefarious and unforeseen malevolent forces at play that undermined what was to be Hillary's triumphal return to the White House. For Hillary supporters, there was no other possible explanation for her loss.

Thus began the Russian collusion narrative. Trump didn't win the election. He engaged in subterfuge in concert with the Russians to steal it from Hillary.

CHAPTER FIVE

Roots of the Media's Psychosis

In order to understand fully the psychosis currently gripping the mainstream media, one must first appreciate the enormous effect Trump's upset victory had on the mindset of political journalists. For the media, Trump's electoral triumph wasn't merely the disappointment that ordinarily follows when one's candidate of choice fails to win. It was a seismic event, not only unparalleled in recent American political history, but also, unrivaled in the impact it had on journalists, especially "objective" reporters, who had prostrated themselves before Hillary Clinton during the campaign.

Trump's interfering, or bending the progressive identity politics arc of history in an impermissible direction, was the single most important factor that spurred the tsunami of media criticism and outrage. Every other unflattering characteristic of Trump, every one of his foibles, all, were in the end, irrelevant and purely incidental, as an incitement for the mainstream media's bitterness.

Trump didn't just defeat Hillary, he obstructed the predestined dialectical forces of progressivism. After the epic ascension of Obama, the nation's first black president, history decreed this was to be followed by the inexorable election of the First.Woman. President.

Many left-leaning publications could not understand why all Americans didn't embrace this implacable march of history. Brittany M. Hughes, writing in the Media Research Center, explained this none-of-my-friends-voted-for-Trump myopia,

> "The front page of the left-leaning Huffington Post didn't shy away from what its publishers thought about Tuesday's election. Stark, bold letters emblazoned on HuffPo's homepage screamed, "Mourning in America: NIGHTMARE: Prez Trump... America Elected A Man Who Said 'Grab Them By The Pu**y' Over The First Female President... Party Ends In Tears..." Poor HuffPo seemed downright stunned that any voter would choose Trump over Clinton and her "history-making story arc."[1]

There were many other twisted identity politics responses to Trump's victory on the part of left-wing publications,"Over at Mother Jones, writers seemed flabbergasted that anyone would vote for a man over a woman and deny females a chance to make history, touting an editorial entitled "Hate Trumps History: A Reality TV Star Wins the White House in a Broken America."[2]

Thus, for the political media elite, the greatest infraction for which Trump must atone was derailing the gender-centric candidacy of the first woman president. Nothing else Trump did or said throughout the campaign or on election night warranted the obloquy of the press corps as much as this unforgivable sin. Journalists would make certain that Trump's malfeasance did not go unpunished. The media was intent on exacting its pound of flesh from this interloper.

Since beating Hillary was a grievous offense, not only would journalists and cable TV commentators berate the man who had vanquished Hillary, but also, those voters who were responsible for putting the gate-crasher in the Oval Office became the object of the slander campaign in which the media dutifully engaged.

A condescending Christiane Amanpour, was saddened to learn of the unwashed masses unenlightened decision to vote for Trump. How could those who voted for Trump be so ignorant as not to see the only choice was Hillary?,

> "So yes, like so many around the world, I was shocked -- very few ever imagined that so many Americans conducting their sacred duty in the sanctity of the voting booth, with their secret ballot, would be angry enough to ignore the wholesale

> vulgarity of language, the sexual predatory behavior, the deep misogyny, the bigoted and insulting view."[3]

The media utterly failed to convince long-term Democrats and former Obama voters in the heartland to vote for Hillary. Now, those redneck know-nothings would be taught a lesson. After all, as MSNBC morning host Mika Bresinski noted, it is "our job," not Trump's, to "control exactly what people think." In the end, the only people who listened to the pleas of journalists not to vote for Donald Trump, were other mainstream media journalists.

Trump's resounding victory demonstrated definitively, the impotence of the political media in terms of changing voters preferences. Those days are over and the mainstream media is reacting with fury to their inability to shape public opinion in the "right direction."

The political media's Trump campaign strategy backfired, causing even more delirium after Trump's victory, because of the realization that in the end, they had been duped. The free air time strategy of the mainstream media made sense during the primaries, because Trump was going to lose, so the media didn't need to worry about inadvertently assisting his campaign. Besides, the traveling Trump show was good for ratings.

But, when he actually WON, all their plans were for naught and they came to the stark realization that it was Trump who had played them for fools, not vice versa. The media's free air time strategy had ignominiously backfired.

And, the blunder cost them dearly. As Jay Caruso of Red State noted at the time, "The figure given is Trump was given about $2 billion in free advertising. It was only until Trump got the nomination that the media realized, "Oh crap. Look what we helped do!" Suddenly, speaking truth to power was important."[4]

The candidate who journalists jokingly treated as a novelty item and circus clown had turned the tables on complacent members of the media. Their arrogance, made them certain they had made Trump a target, when in fact, it was he, who had long ago during the primaries, put a bullseye on their backs.

Trump's victory also induced a collective state of stupefaction among members of the media because their predictions and expectations were so thoroughly flawed.

Yet, instead of providing the occasion for introspection and an honest assessment of the reasons why the smartest woman in the world was bested by a political neophyte, the media and Hillary supporters instead exploded into public expressions of convulsions.

The amount that was at stake for servile members of the media in a second Clinton presidency was enormous. Loyal and sycophantic "reporters" such as Amy Chozick would be handsomely rewarded in a Hillary Clinton Administration with access to the president (an occasion, above all else, for more fawning interviews) and exclusive stories. For members of the media these would be career boosters.

After Trump's upset victory, imagine the horror and shock visited upon senior media officials, reporters and craven journalists who had shamelessly consorted with the Clinton campaign, as though Hillary was a sure thing. When the bomb exploded, there were no foxholes in which to hide.

CHAPTER SIX

No Honeymoon For Trump

A telling example representative of the insanity that engulfed the pundit class shellshocked by Hillary's loss was Richard Cohen's *Washington Post* column, written on January 10, 2017, ten days before Trump's inauguration. Cohen was beside himself over Trump's election,

> "Donald Trump is a one-man basket of deplorables. He is a braggart and a liar. He is a bully and a demagogue. He is an ignoramus and a deadbeat, a chiseler and either a sincere racist or an insincere one, and his love for himself is matched only by my loathing of him. He is about to be president of the United States."[1]

But, Cohen was just getting warmed up. A constitutional coup may be in the offing, Cohen gravely intoned. And the grounds for such a draconian measure? "Trump has not moderated his behavior. He still behaves like a brat — his childish tweet zinging Arnold Schwarzenegger for failing to get Trumpian ratings on "The New Celebrity Apprentice" being the most amusing example."[2]

Trump hadn't sufficiently moderated his behavior to conform to Cohen's strict requirements for presidential decorum and as such, needed to be removed from office. One wonders what the easily offended Cohen had to say about Bill Clinton's predatory behavior while he was actually in the White House.

For his fellow journalists, Cohen's inconsistency was immaterial. Since all standards and journalistic principles were abandoned for reporting and commenting on the Trump Administration, hypocrisy was no longer a vice, but rather, a virtue.

Since impeachment was too laborious a remedy for ridding the world of Trump, Cohen endorsed and encouraged employing the 25th Amendment, because it was manifestly clear to Cohen, that Trump was unfit for the office he would soon hold and needs to be "constrained", if necessary, by his own cabinet.

Had a conservative writer written a similarly venomous column about the newly elected Barack Obama, he would have been forced to flee for his life, mindful of staying one step ahead of a crowd of irate journalists brandishing pitchforks and screaming "Racist!"

That Marty Baron, editor of the Post, could say with a straight face, one month after Cohen's diatribe, that the Post was not biased, shows the utter disconnect between the Beltway media and the rest of the country. How Baron could print such a disturbing unedited opinion piece in his paper, is indicative of his unbridled disdain for the new president of the United States. Baron merely confirmed what for years has been an indisputable fact: *The Washington*

Post is a newspaper for the Democratic Party. Many of its commentators, such as the execrable Dana Milbank, yes, the same Milbank who asked the Clinton campaign for opposition research for one of his articles, are nothing more than left wing partisan hacks.

Writing in *Hot Air*, Jazz Shaw describes the Post's terminal incapacity for self-examination:

> "Just in case you were wondering whether the owners of the Washington Post learned anything from the last election and their failure to stop America from voting for Donald Trump, fear not. They haven't. If there was any sort of change coming to the editorial board, they probably wouldn't have given a green light to Richard Cohen's column this week which carries the not very ambiguous title of, "How to remove Trump from office."[3]

Those who don't believe the pre-inauguaration attacks on Trump by the media were unwarranted or biased, would be well advised to harken back eight years ago and review the commentary by journalists concerning Obama, a/k/a, "The One", who was going to halt the rise of the oceans and heal the planet. Unlike the incessant rage visited upon Trump, before Obama set foot in the Oval Office, the veneration shown for the New Messiah was positively effusive and cringe-worthy.

A few examples will suffice for those who have trouble understanding why so many Americans hold the Mainstream Media-Democratic Party-Complex in such low esteem. Illustrative of the hosannahs showered upon the mainstream media's New Messiah, was the comment of Evan Thomas, a Newsweek editor, who referred to Obama as, "a sort of God."

Before Obama had set foot in the Oval Office, some historians were already comparing favorably the president-elect and former community organizer with the august Abraham Lincoln.

But the praises began well before he won the election.

In 2007, a day after Obama announced his candidacy, then *Washington Post* media critic

Howard Kurtz, found the Obama exaltations pushed to the extremes,

"I haven't seen a politician get this kind of walk-on-water coverage since Colin Powell a dozen years ago flirted with making a run for the White House," Kurtz noted.[4] The benedictions bestowed upon Obama began to resemble religious fervor. Kurtz further elaborated, "I mean, it is amazing . . . a guy with all of two years' experience in the United States Senate getting coverage that ranges from positive to glowing to even gushing."[5]

And, saving the best for last, was the notorious and positively nauseating paean penned by Mark Morford of the *San Francisco Chronicle*,

> "Many spiritually advanced people I know . . . identify Obama as a Lightworker, that rare kind of attuned being who has the ability to lead us not merely to new foreign policies or health care plans or whatnot, but who can actually help usher in a new way of being on the planet, of relating and connecting and engaging with this bizarre earthly experiment. These kinds of people actually help us evolve. They are philosophers and peacemakers of a

> very high order, and they speak not just to reason or emotion, but to the soul."[6]

Ten years later, the media deification of Obama appears quite ridiculous and in light of his two years in the U.S. Senate, completely unwarranted; the Lincoln comparisons, risible. Once Trump vanquished Hillary, journalists redirected the intensity of their over-the-top praise for Obama, converted that enthusiasm into vitriol and then unleashed it, with a fury, at the anti-Obama.

Any honest person, regardless of political affiliation, must acknowledge the difference in treatment afforded the two president-elects, is simply astounding, regardless of the unique and historical nature of Obama's candidacy.

These examples of Obama-worship are important for an understanding of the relationship between Trump and the media, for they help explain the transformation of political journalists opinions of Trump from mere disapprobation during the primaries, to unprecedented vilification once he beat Hillary.

Once elected, journalists realized, much to their chagrin, that Trump was going to rescind some of the signature policies of their demi-god.

In a breach of long established decorum, an ungracious, malevolent and irate media, still smarting from the dethroning of the First. Woman. President., began to excoriate Trump before he had set foot in the Oval Office. What happened to the Trump honeymoon? As Matthew Continetti observed,

> "The opposition has long granted presidents time to form their administrations, to announce their signature initiatives. Donald Trump's honeymoon lasted all of 10 days—from his surprise November 8 election to the rude treatment of his vice president at a performance of Hamilton on November 18. After that, divorce."[7]

As a sampling of the extraordinary impertinence exhibited towards the newly sworn-in president, consider this impudent and contemptible op-ed penned by one Rosa Parks, a hard left, ex-Obama Administration State Department official and a law professor. In a wondrous moment of intellectual splendor,

Professor Parks, with her inquiring mind and progressive perspicuity, wanted to know,

> "Are we really stuck with this guy? It's the question being asked around the globe, because Donald Trump's first week as president has made it all too clear: Yes, he is as crazy as everyone feared."[8]

Parks then proceeded to argue, in an incoherent manner, that Trump should be removed through impeachment, by invoking the 25th Amendment, or, if necessary, by a military coup, should in her opinion, Trump issue an unlawful order.

Had a law professor from Georgetown called for the impeachment or removal of Barack Obama, does anyone doubt that individual would be immediately dismissed? Liberal pundits would characterize such a comment as a call for insurrection against the nation's first black president.

The ideas penned by Parks in her inflammatory article were embraced wholeheartedly by the media; her calls for impeachment and the use of the 25th amendment were endlessly discussed on the cable talk shows. Such ideas and commentary were viewed as legitimate —even necessary — because, after all, as Parks and so many others had concluded, the president was crazy, a menace to the country and unfit to serve.

It is instructive to note that Parks penned her commentary exactly ten days after Trump's inauguration. Parks disabused those who foolishly harbored the illusion, that even Trump, should be afforded a honeymoon, however brief.

The Mainstream Media-Democratic Party-Complex ratified Parks extremism and it became the rallying cry for members of the Resistance.

The media eagerly stoked such 25th amendment nonsense. Pundits, alleged legal "experts" commentators and some Democratic politicians enthusiastically embraced the preposterous ideas bandied about for Trump's removal.

"Conservative" columnist for the *New York Times*, neverTrumper, Ross Douthat, joined the chorus of those who claimed that the president should be removed by way of the 25th amendment, Douthat concluded, along with so many other elites, both anti-Trump Republicans and Democrats alike, that Trump does not,"sufficiently understands the nature of the office he holds, the nature of the legal constraints that are supposed to bind him, perhaps even the nature of normal human interactions, to be guilty of obstruction of justice in the Nixonian or even Clintonian sense of the phrase."[9]

After Trump's inauguration, the battle lines immediately were drawn between the president and his antagonists in the media. Unlike the honeymoon Obama enjoyed with the media — which evolved into an unbroken eight-year love affair —there would be not even the slightest period of goodwill or cordiality extended to this president.

No other president in recent memory, including the thoroughly reviled Richard Nixon, was treated with such disdain and disrespect as that visited upon Donald Trump as soon as he entered the Oval Office.

Part Three
Media Assault on the Trump Administration

CHAPTER SEVEN

Formation of the Resistance

After recovering from the immediate jolt and stupor she experienced late in the evening on November 7th, Hillary gradually emerged from her post-election coma. Sipping Chardonnay and long walks in the woods near the Clinton's Chappaqua residence helped her cope.[1] Nonetheless, the wine couldn't eliminate the torpor and the disbelief that lingered, as Hillary tried to process how she, a woman destined for a rendezvous with history, could be dethroned by a reality TV star. It was like the Japanese sneak attack on Pearl Harbor: no one saw it coming, because no one would have believed it possible.

Emotionally distraught over her loss, Hillary's bewildered loyal supporters, often times would burst out in tears. Rebecca Traister, an impassioned Hillary fan, assures us that these incidents of weeping in public were real, as it wasn't just Hillary who endured a sense of loss,

> "Almost everywhere Clinton goes, it seems, someone starts crying. It's not just friends and staffers. And though it was more intense in the weeks immediately following the election, it hasn't entirely let up. At restaurants, in grocery stores, on planes, and in the woods, there are lines of people wanting selfies, hugs, comfort."[2]

Hillary stoked her self-pity with concocted tales of frequent expressions of dismay from her traumatized disciples, who seemed to appear in public, wherever she went, witless and with heavy hearts,

> "It's been unlike anything I've ever seen," she says. "I mean, it doesn't end. Every time I'm in public. I was having lunch with Shonda Rhimes last week and a woman stopped at the table — well-dressed, probably in her 40s or 50s — and she said, 'I just

can't leave this restaurant without telling you I'm just so devastated,' and she just started to cry."

In such cases, Hillary was always there to console her disheartened admirers,

> "I was on the other side of the table, or I would have done what I have done countless times since the election, which is just put my arms around her. Because people are so profoundly hurt. And it is, yes, predominantly women. But men say it in a different way. Men are, 'I voted for you and I don't know what the hell happened.' But for women who supported me or who feel bad that they didn't, not because they voted for somebody else but because they didn't vote[3] …"

This post-election fairy tale gained traction with each passing day. As the undocumented reports of frequent fits of public wailing by her dejected fans demonstrated, the stinging repudiation Hillary suffered was surely due to sinister forces, rather than her corruption and inauthenticity.

The persistent and nagging question for Hillary and her supplicant supporters, including the mainstream media, then became, what malevolent and devious force intervened to derail her trail-blazing quest for the presidential brass ring.

Hillary's post-election anguish, would eventually ferment into a pathetic and delusional display of denial, blame shifting and conniving, to create a Russia/Trump fable that she hoped would vindicate her misapprehension that she didn't lose, but rather, the election was stolen from her. Only a woman with a colossal sense of entitlement could project such phony pathos.

Trump's election had the unintended, but enlightening, effect of exposing the worst traits of the three main modern-day pillars of the Left: the Democratic Party, the mainstream media and academia. The initial trauma this triumvirate of liberalism suffered when Hillary was defeated was later supplanted by anger and then subsequently, a descent into madness that took the form of Trump Derangement Syndrome.

Media, academia and the Democratic Party were inextricably conjoined after the election, unified with an assiduity of purpose towards one goal: to derail Trump's presidency.

Henceforth, all reporting on Trump would universally adopt the principles of The Narrative. Germinated in the left-wing fringes of academia, the Narrative began to flourish under Obama, was embraced later by the Democratic Party and then subsequently adopted by the mainstream media. The maxims of the Narrative as they applied to the Trump presidency can be summarized in the following proposition: Trump is dangerous and unstable. Trump and his supporters are irredeemable racists, misogynists, white nationalists, xenophobes, etc. etc., etc…

After the election, the Mainstream Media-Democratic Party-Complex would dutifully report on the Trump Administration in accordance with these new and unwavering "iron laws" of journalism. From the moment he defeated the smartest woman in the world, nearly every media attack against Trump contained a number of common attributes:

Iron Laws For Journalists In the Age of Trump:

1. All Reporting on the Trump Administration must follow and advance The Narrative;

2. Trump is manifestly unfit for the presidency and represents a danger to the Republic;

3. Vilify Trump in the harshest possible manner for committing the exact same infractions as Obama;

4. Deliberately and maliciously, omit to state material facts about a story or report that would make the statements made in the article or report not misleading;

5. Dispense with all standards of journalism;

6. Interpret every policy position or response of the Trump Administration on important issues such as immigration, as

motivated solely by racism and white nationalism;

7. Denigrate all Trump supporters as irredeemable racists;

8. Denigrate all Trump supporters as misogynists;

9. Denigrate all Trump supporters as xenophobes;

10. Denigrate all Trump supporters as Islamaphobes;

11. Denigrate all Trump supporters as white nationalists; and,

12. Explain Trump's policy differences with Obama as motivated purely by racism, Islamophobism, misogony, white nationalism, Nazism, White privilege and xenophobism;, lather, wash, rinse, repeat…

CHAPTER EIGHT
The Russian Collusion Chimera

Immediately after the election, there were heated discussions amongst Clinton's campaign staff and a lot of finger pointing. In order to assuage the pain of her stunning loss, Hillary began to proffer the theory or narrative, that she lost the election due to a surge in White Nationalism as well as collusion between Trump and the Russians. Ludicrous as this fanciful explanation may have been, it would form the underpinnings of a diabolical and cynical scheme, enthusiastically embraced by the Mainstream Media-Democratic Party-Complex, that would prove inimical to Trump's presidency. Jonathan and Amy Parnes, authors of *Shattered: Inside Hillary Clinton's Doomed Campaign*, recount the blame game initiated by Hillary, "A few days after the election, Hillary was less accepting of her defeat. She put a fine point on the factors she believed cost her the presidency: the FBI(Comey), the KGB and the KKK (the support Trump got from White Nationalists)."[1]

In a state of stupefaction over her shocking defeat, Hillary refused to accept blame for her defeat, "In other calls with advisers and political surrogates in the days the election, Hillary declined to take responsibility for her own loss. "She's not being particularly self-reflective," in the words of one longtime ally who was on calls with her shortly after the election."[2]

Hillary's steadfast refusal to accept any responsibility for her defeat, made the atmosphere of post-election meetings with staff ripe for a convenient conspiracy theory, "Instead, Hillary kept pointing her finger at Comey and Russia. " She wants to make sure all these narratives get spun the right way, this person said."[3]

It is crucial to note, that despite Hillary's increasingly strident strategy of blaming others for her loss, there was a brief, but nonetheless illuminating moment of candor among some campaign staff the day after the thunderclap struck. Some aides in a rare moment of honesty acknowledged that, "It was a mismanaged campaign from the start, 150 percent," one aide said. "There was so much stuff that needed fixing. I thought we might have learned some lessons from the primary. But as you can tell from last night, probably not."[4]

Given this admission of gross negligence on the part of the Clinton campaign, it is utterly astonishing the ease with which a compliant media swallowed whole Hillary's audacious Russians-stole-the-election nonsense. There is no post-election blight on the mainstream media more egregious, than this abandonment of journalistic skepticism.

This frank acknowledgment of Clinton's screw-up by her own campaign advisors however, would be of no consequence for a woman aggrieved. Continuing her state of perpetual denial, Hillary, with the able assistance from an army of sycophants, convinced herself she had committed no blunders during the campaign.

This devious stratagem to deflect blame from herself and by implication, her campaign staff, gained acceptance shortly after the election. The Russia "narrative" would exonerate Hillary and shift the blame for her loss to Russian interference in the election. Her accomplices in the media would disseminate the story. "That strategy had been set within twenty-four hours of her concession speech. Mook and Podesta assembled her communications team at the Brooklyn headquarters to engineer the case that the election wasn't entirely on the up-and-up.

The Russian/Trump contrivance was prepared for Hillary's lap dogs in the media for dissemination to the public. "For a couple of hours, with Shake Shack containers littering the room, they went over the script they would pitch to the press and the pubic. Already, Russian hacking was the centerpiece of the argument."[5]

It is a stinging indictment of the political media, that there were no curious reporters willing to pursue a story about Hillary's weaving a deceitful yarn that she and her staff knew would seriously hamper and undermine Trump's presidency before he had even assumed the office. Hillary's Russia collusion machinations were hardly secret, as after *Shattered* was published, the book became the talk of the town.

The revelations contained in the last chapter of *Shattered*, described a dastardly and knowing fabrication of a story intended to harm and question the legitimacy of the newly elected president. The book was replete with explosive details about a conscious effort by a losing candidate to maliciously sow the seed that would occasion doubt about whether the election was above-board. Only a press corps that was so thoroughly vested in her victory could in unison, give a collective shrug over the damning details published in this widely anticipated and widely circulated book.

Journalists were too busy grieving to investigate and report on this story about how a serpentine Hillary, in concert with her campaign staff, looking to parry blame for their gross negligence for the political upset of the century, had no compunction about floating a baseless story about imaginary Trump/Russia duplicity.

There was nary a word discussed about the effects this might have on the young Trump Administration, nor the obvious fallout from such a false and malicious narrative on the body-politic.

Floating the Russian collusion narrative was Hillary at her worst: dissembling, conniving, paired with a pathological inability to accept responsibility for her mistakes. Disseminating the Russia story to a compliant media eager to accept it was an act of remarkable chutzpah; shameless, even for a woman who had no shame.

What is also striking about the incurious press corps was the knowledge that the basis on which the FBI obtained a FISA warrant to spy on the Trump campaign was the Steele dossier — a document paid for by Hillary's campaign. Where was the "free" press while this story was developing? Where were all those crack Pulitzer Prize winning investigative journalists and reporters at the *New York Times*, especially Hillary fan, Amy Chozik?

MIA, every last one.

It is of great significance to note that not only did the media deliberately ignore a story of Watergate proportions, it played an indispensable role in facilitating the counterfeit Russia collusion story.

As was made abundantly clear by the WikiLeaks email disclosures, because of the symbiosis between the Clinton campaign and the media during the election, Hillary's fabricating the Russia story was significant because the media had no choice but to carry Hillary's water on the collusion narrative.

When Trump won, journalists looked idiotic, every bit as foolish as Clinton and completely out of touch with the world outside of Washington. The salvation for the mainstream media for their colossal blunder in missing the rise of Trump lay in perpetuating the Russian collusion story after Hillary initially planted the seed. Journalists would cultivate Hillary's mythical tale into a delusional and unrelenting narrative that would eventually lead to the mainstream media's descent into madness and its ultimate demise.

Because the media had a vested interest in proselytizing the nonsense Hillary was spoon-feeding them, once the dust from the election settled, its relationship with the Trump Administration was predestined to be one of hostility and confrontation.

We now know of course, that it was Hillary's campaign that paid a retired British spy, Christopher Steele, to go to Russia for the sole purpose of concocting a tale of Trump campaign collusion with Russia. The Steele dossier was a wholly fabricated document rife with speculations, double hearsay, falsehoods and outright lies. One such story had Trump urinating on the hotel bed where Obama stayed in Russia. The dossier was later used as a basis to obtain a FISA warrant to spy on the Trump campaign.

Hillary's gambit was wildly successful and perfectly complimented her whirlwind tour to pitch her new book. The Steele dossier was the proximate cause for the appointment of a special counsel, Robert Mueller.

After her adept planting of the Russian collusion idea, the media followed in lock-step and in a display of unrelenting tenacity would make this ruse the central topic that would dominate their reporting on the Trump Administration.

Not one prominent media outlet questioned the source of the Steele dossier, the veracity of its underlying assumptions and the Clinton campaign's inextricable association with the former British spy who was paid by Hillary and who submitted this story to the FBI, the intelligence agencies and the media, all with the singular purpose of defeating a political opponent during a presidential election.

Hillary's fomenting the Russia bogeyman through her campaign's payments to a thoroughly discredited ex-British spy was pure Clintonian genius: dissembling, deflection and deceit all conceived by a woman who had years of political experience using the same odious tactics against her and her husband's enemies. The Clintons had many years experience manipulating the media and their proficiency was on display.

The media assisted in giving Hillary's phantasmagoria legs when they failed to report on what was perhaps one of the most salient facts concerning the chimera of Trump/Russian collusion: that the attempts at election interference were well known by the Obama Administration. Michael Goodwin of the *New York Post* perspicaciously noted the galling hypocrisy and misdirection employed by the mainstream media to exonerate and shield Obama from any blame, "For all the focus on Russia, the media totally missed a key point. To wit, that the Obama administration did nothing about Vladimir Putin's attempt to interfere in the 2016 election even though the White House knew about it for months."[6]

That is to say, for the media, the only Russia angle worth reporting was the one that supported Hillary's post-election explanation for her loss: the wholly unfounded, fact-free idea that Trump in concert with Putin robbed Hillary of her rightful crown. The craven media wholeheartedly embraced the story.

CHAPTER NINE
Media Merges Into the Resistance

The reason the crescendo of opposition to Trump was so deafening and incessant was that his winning the presidency rattled all the prominent institutions of liberalism: the media, the Washington political elite, the entertainment industry and left-wing fringe academics that were assuming an increasingly prominent role in the messaging for the Democratic Party. Each of these prongs of the liberal Democratic Party establishment, that had enjoyed unquestioned prominence under Obama, coalesced around one goal: the derailment of the Trump presidency.

Mainstream Media Democratic Party Complex

The effort to drive Trump from office was implemented with an tenacity of purpose and fanatic zeal. As soon as Trump made it clear that he would not bow down nor cower before a political media that had been acclimated to decades of compliant Republicans, a veritable siege or bunker mentality was set in motion by the players who had long called the shots in the nation's capitol. For the Mainstream Media-Democratic Party-Complex, the die was cast and the battle joined.

It should come as no surprise, that since Trump had been repeatedly compared to Hitler (yes, the madman who exterminated millions and had Buchenwald and Treblinka constructed), zany, left-wing academics, cable TV commentators and liberal pundits, in a profound and appalling demonstration of their historical ignorance, all began to use other WWII Nazi imagery, their favorite being to liken Trump's addresses to his supporters as "Nuremberg" rallies.

In the hierarchy of the Resistance, anti-Trumpers were bestowed exalted status: they were the 21st century equivalent of the heroic French Resistance fighters planning underground raids on the occupation Trump Administration. At no other time in American History, have the politically vanquished, encouraged by the mainstream media, be-clowned themselves in such a manner.

After Hillary adroitly planted the seed for the Russian collusion story, her demented supporters latched on to this nascent narrative willingly stoked by the Mainstream Media-Democratic Party-Complex.

The plan was to flaunt the explosive bombshell Russia collusion story, that over time, would remove Trump from office and vindicate Hillary and her media lackeys that her majesty did not in fact, lose the election, but rather it was stolen from her — making Trump's presidency illegitimate.

The Russia/Trump myth started to gain legs after the election; with each passing day it gained further momentum. By the time of Trump's inauguration, there were those calling for his impeachment.

It is indisputable that no other president in modern history had been the object of such antipathy from the press corps as Trump. The invective leveled at Trump from the media only worked to heighten the public's awareness of their manifest bias. Victor Davis Hanson observed that Trump's election, "has redefined the American media by stripping nearly all pretenses off its once carefully sculpted disinterested veneer. In other words, never before in American presidential history—not even during the dark days of Watergate—have the media so despised a sitting president.[1]"

The formation of the Resistance was indicative of the fact that the Democrats and their media allies genuinely believed that Trump represented an "occupation" Administration that needed to be harassed by underground methods. Partisan tactics would take the form of bureaucratic civil disobedience (e.g., Sally

Yates' feigned moral stance on refusing to implement Trump's lawful travel ban order) or through open and persistent press attacks on the legitimacy of his presidency, much in the same way the French viewed the Germans as unwanted, illicit and oppressive occupiers.

Trump's antagonists in the media viewed him as nothing more than a 21st century version of Marshal Petain, the head of the much-loathed Vichy government.

The entire "Resistance" movement evoked ridiculous images of beltway political journalists, disaffected Hillary supporters and anti-Trump Republicans all adorned with black berets, crouched over a table in the basement of a farmhouse in Northern France; Sten guns at the ready, chain-smoking Gauloises, listening intently to the evening BBC shortwave broadcast for a coded message signaling the allied invasion on the coast of ~~Normandy~~ Mar-a-Lago was imminent.

Vive La France!! Vive La Resistance!

No other president in the history of the Republic has had to endure such patent nonsense, not even the much-reviled Richard Nixon. History will record these pathetic media-enabled "Resistance" antics during the immediate post-election period as an exercise in monumental silliness.

CHAPTER TEN
Media Makes Themselves the News

Since it functioned as the opposition party, the media became the spearhead for the Resistance. It inveighed daily against the norms of the new Administration, paramount of which was Trump's lack of respect for an institution that fancied itself a free press serving nobly as a bulwark against executive abuses of power.

One of the most hyperbolic of all the Resistance end-of-the-world warnings about threats to press freedom, came from CNN reporter, Christiane Amanpour, who said,

> "I never in a million years thought I would be up here on stage appealing for the freedom and safety of American journalists at home."[1] These are difficult

> times for America's journalists", Amanpour explained plaintively. "Since the dawn of the 2016 presidential campaign, reporters have been harassed, threatened and even arrested and charged with felonies for simply doing their jobs."

For Amanpour, Trump's election was an ominous event and threat to a free press because, he riled up crowds of his supporters against the media at his Nuremberg-style rallies. Amanpour somberly warned of additional and unprecedented threats to a free press, such as,"…ordering journalists not to film the daily presidential briefings." This unexampled proposal represents, "another brick in the wall that Team Trump is constructing against press freedom."[2]

Amanpour's tirade was preposterous. Not only was Trump whipping up crowds of his racist, white nationalist supporters, in frightening Nuremberg style rallies, worse still, he was planning on removing cameras from the daily presidential briefings, which meant her colleague at CNN, the insufferable Jim Acosta, wouldn't be able to preen before his peers.

Amanpour's grave concern for the freedom and safety of journalists in the new dark age of Trump was comical, when one realizes that when Obama actually did threaten to jail journalists, Amanpour spoke nary a word.

The media's constant whining that Trump declared war on a free press is farcical as well as duplicitous when the unvarnished facts revealed that Trump was merely following a trail blazed by Obama in undermining openness and press freedom. Trump's alleged infractions against the press were simply borrowed from his predecessor, who was in many ways infinitely more hostile to the Fourth Estate.

This is a splendid example of Iron Law # 3 in action: Vilify Trump in the harshest possible manner for committing the exact same infractions as Obama.

How did Trump's "unprecedented" assault against press freedom compare to the practices employed by his exalted forerunner? An analysis reveals that in terms of attacking the press, Trump was a rank amateur compared to Obama.

Here is a list of the assaults against press freedom carried out by the media's New Messiah, as noted by Julie Mason of the Houston Chronicle:[3]

During his presidency:

1. Obama frequently blocked news photographers' from official functions, maintaining exclusive access for the president's own PR massagers;

2. President Obama rarely fielded questions from reporters and went months between press conferences, opting instead for one-on-one interviews with mostly friendly anchors that allowed him more control;

3. Obama broke his campaign pledge to make his schedule public and his staff frequently scrubbed public visitor logs to conceal the names of White House visitors;

4. The Obama administration substantially impeded Freedom of Information Act processing, compiling the worst record in history for fulfilling requests from citizens and journalists alike for access to public records;

5. The Obama Justice Department in 2013, seized phone records of the Associated Press, surreptitiously collections information from 20 phone lines of reporters and editors, these included cell, work and home phones;

6. Obama used federal prosecutors to go after news sources. After campaigning as a reformer who would protect whistleblowers, Obama made greater use of the Espionage Act to prosecute leakers and menace journalists than all other presidents combined; and

7. Obama's Justice Department in 2010 infiltrated the private email of Fox News reporter James Rosen, who was reporting on North Korea. The

administration also seized personal records from Rosen's colleagues and parents.

Here is a question that ought to be posed to Christiane Amanpour, Jim Acosta, as well as Dean Baquet and Jim Rutenberg of the *New York Times*. Why no criticism of Obama for his truly unprecedented assault on press freedoms, when Trump was merely following his lead?

In light of Obama's many instances of actually circumscribing press freedoms, the diffidence expressed by Christiane Amanpour, over Trump's election, devolves from the sublime to the ridiculous.

Once the Washington political media determined its moral obligation to oppose the newly elected president superseded all the once-respected tenets of journalism, whenever Trump justifiably attacked reporters, cries of press freedom being in jeopardy were soon to follow. In short, once they paired with the Resistance, the media made themselves the news.

After the shock of the election had subsided, journalists proudly announced to the public their newfound intention to speak "truth to power" in order to hold a menacing and unorthodox president Trump accountable. Full of self-importance, Lloyd Grove boasted, "Journalism is back. In a big way."[4]

Writing in National Review, historian Varad Mehta described this orgy of self-congratulation,

> "Immediately after the election, members of the media began issuing birth announcements like proud new parents. "On November 9, Margaret Sullivan of the *Washington Post* exhorted her allies to marshal their forces: "We have to keep doing our jobs of truth-telling, challenging power and holding those in power accountable. We have to be willing to fight back." The time had come "to toughen up and be as good as we can be, all of us."[5]

Other journalists who had joined the Resistance announced, through ridiculous expressions of self-esteem, their intention to follow suit,

> "In January, *Politico's* Jack Shafer failed to see his shadow and prophesied that Trump's inauguration heralded the advent of "journalistic spring." Similar proclamations abounded, from the New Year's resolution by the *New York Times'* Nick Kristof, who vowed that the press would be "watchdogs, not lap dogs," to the promise by Vox founder Ezra Klein that his outlet would cover the new president "by focusing on policy, and the people affected." Journalists lined up to affirm that they felt reenergized, reinvigorated, and filled with a renewed sense of purpose.[6]"

This insufferable sanctimony was indicative of an institution that was so clueless, that it completely escaped their attention (but no one else's) that if the media was undergoing a Renaissance, how did they explain the Dark Ages that preceded the rebirth? Mehta notes,

> "There is no answer to this question that casts the media in a flattering light. At best, they were merely derelict; at worst, they refused to do their job for reasons of politics and partisanship. It's unlikely that in their hosannas to themselves, reporters meant to convey the impression that hitherto they had been asleep at the switch.[7]"

Indeed, most Americans asked the same questions. Given the love affair between Barack

Obama and the Washington press corps for the past eight years, the question raised when speaking of a Renaissance answers itself: journalism took a hiatus for the term of the Obama Administration. Many historians and pundits claimed he was the smartest president ever to grace Pennsylvania Avenue —before he spent a day in the White House. And, the most endearing of all the praise: he was going to be august, like Lincoln, another tribute made before Obama had sat at his desk in the Oval Office.

During Obama's presidency, journalists cast aside their duty to hold high public officials accountable for their abuses of power and other violations of the public trust. Since they saw it as their sacred duty to assist in electing the nation's first African-American president, they all had a vested interest in assuring his presidency was successful, or at least not diminished by scandal or instances of abuse of power.

There were numerous and serious instances of corruption during the Obama presidency that ordinarily would have had any marginally competent journalist scrambling to cover it in depth for their Pulitzer nomination. Yet, instead, the media, who never tire of telling us of their indispensable role in a democracy as the principal bulwark against tyranny as well as holding the powerful accountable, were on an extended leave of absence during the Obama presidency.

When these same fearless members of the Fourth Estate, full of self-importance, began reporting critically on Trump, a question arose: where were these intrepid journalists during the Obama presidency? The answer is that they were missing in action. The list of abuses of power under Obama's tenure was long: Fast and Furious, the gross incompetence and criminal negligence bureaucrats at the Veterans Administration, the use of the IRS as a political weapon to silence conservative opponents and the unprecedented politicization of the Justice

Department. How about the deceitfulness in connection with the enactment of Obamacare: "If you like your doctor, you can keep your doctor."

None of these violations of the public trust warranted so much as a collective yawn on the part of the Fourth Estate. By their unswerving devotion and ingratiating loyalty to the Obama Administration, journalists willingly threw away what little was left of their credibility and integrity.

As Mollie Hemingway wrote, "…A media that doesn't push back against that type of falsehood for eight years and then gets all upset at Sean Spicer talking about numbers is not going to be taken seriously at all.[8]" They betrayed their profession and their responsibilities and they wonder why when Trump attacks them as hypocrites and overtly biased the crowds spontaneously and wildly cheer.

After the election, members of the press corps shed their reporters hat and enthusiastically joined the Resistance and in the process, forever tarnished their reputation. Victor Davis Hanson noted the significance, "The effort to remove the president is conducted by the *New York Times*, *The Washington Post*, the wire services, and the major networks. And we have seen nothing like it in our time Hanson said." The number of patently false and defamatory reports published by the media as "Breaking News", were mounting. "In the last six months, Americans have been told quite falsely so many untruths about the Trump administration by their news agencies that for all practical purposes, there is no such thing as a media as we once knew it."[9]

A Trump presidency was so perilous for the health of the Republic as well as the news business, that James Rutenberg of the *New York Times*, reminded journalists that they should feel no need to treat the exceptional Trump candidacy by "normal standards." Trump would be opposed by the virtuous forces of partial journalists, all in the service of the greater good: the defeat of Donald Trump.

CHAPTER ELEVEN
A Malignant Presidency

Shortly after Trump's inauguration, political journalists and the Resistance movement became inseparable. They shared a common identity and a common purpose: remove Trump, a dangerous encroacher, from office using any means necessary, even if it entailed fabricating stories out of whole cloth. Many of the nonsensical claims peddled by a thoroughly corrupt media were bereft of any credible evidence. Did journalists truly believe that Trump, while in Russia, would urinate on the hotel bed where Obama had previously stayed?

Even for those imbued with "Get-Trump" rage, this story should have triggered immediate skepticism. The fact that it didn't, is one of the reasons the public no longer has any faith in journalists ability, or desire, to report the news accurately.

The media and disaffected Hillary supporters (synonymous terms), took their marching orders from the DNC and embraced the concept that their traditional role as reporters, now needed to be enhanced to that of shape-shifters and news massagers in order to exert political influence against the dangerous impulses of the Trump Administration. Victor Davis Hanson describes the post-election epiphany of journalists,

> "The present generation of journalists and reporters tends to believe that just conveying the news no longer offers ample venue for their unappreciated talents, celebrity status, and deserved political influence.
>
> "As a result, they often massage coverage to find relevance as makers, not mere deliverers, of news. Like many academics, writers, and intellectuals of our bicoastal elite landscapes, they are naturally self-

described idealists and left-of-center both politically and culturally.[1]"

An understanding of how the mainstream media radically redefined its traditional role after the election, requires revisiting a pivotal turning point that occurred during the later stages of the 2016 campaign.

In the words of veteran Pulitzer Prize winning journalist, Michael Goodwin, August 7, 2016, was a momentous day in the history of American journalism. It was on this day, that *New York Times* media columnist, James Rutenberg, wrote a provocative and influential article that would henceforth establish, the new rules of journalism in the age of the malevolent and menacing Donald Trump.

On August 7, 2016, after Trump secured the nomination, Rutenberg posed the following question as the general election was underway,

> "If you're a working journalist and you believe that Donald J. Trump is a demagogue playing to the nation's worst racist and nationalistic tendencies, that he cozies up to anti-American dictators and that he

would be dangerous with control of the United States nuclear codes, how the heck are you supposed to cover him?"[2]

As Goodwin noted, before the election of Donald Trump, the answer to that question was self-evident, or at least should have been self-evident,"Under the Times' traditional standards, the right answer is that you wouldn't be allowed to cover any candidate you were so biased against. But that's not the answer Rutenberg gave."[3]

However, after quoting an editor who characterized Hillary as "normal" and Trump "abnormal"," Rutenberg suggested "normal standards" didn't apply. He admitted that "balance has been on vacation" since Trump began to campaign and ended by declaring that it is "journalism's job to be true to the readers and viewers, and true to the facts, in a way that will stand up to history's judgment."[4]

Goodwin characterized the article as a failed attempt to, "justify the lopsided anti-Trump coverage in the Times and other news organizations. It was indeed that — and more, for it also served as a dog whistle for anti-Trump journalists, telling them it was acceptable to reveal their biases."[5]

Shortly after Rutenberg's article, the Times crossed the Rubicon, when executive editor Dean Baquet, enthusiastically supported the "Rutenberg Principle" of partiality, without the slightest reservation, intentionally abandoning any pretense of fairness or objectivity.

Baquet told an interviewer the Rutenberg article "nailed" his thinking and convinced him that the struggle for fairness was over.

"I think that Trump has ended that struggle," Baquet boasted. "I think we now say stuff. We fact-check him. We write it more powerfully that it's false."

Since the Times is the "paper of record" mainstream media journalists could embrace the new standards with a clear conscience.

Banquet's blessing for abandoning elementary principles of journalism, opened the spigot for endless attacks against then candidate Trump. Goodwin elaborated, "Because the Times is the liberal media's bell cow, the floodgates were flung open to routinely call Trump a liar, a racist and a traitor. Standards of fairness were trashed as nearly every prominent news organization demonized Trump and effectively endorsed Clinton. This open partisanship was a disgraceful chapter in the history of American journalism."[6]

All of this was justified because in the words of Watergate has-been, Carl Bernstein, Trump's was a "malignant presidency", words so harsh that they would never have been used to describe even Richard Nixon, the target of Woodward and Bernstein's investigative reporting.

Thus, journalism entered the new post-Trump era that began during the later stages of the election, and continued, once he was elected, for the remainder of his presidency.

When Trump issued his travel ban for countries in the Middle East, he provided the

Mainstream Media Democratic Party Complex

media an occasion to join with academia, federal district court judges and pundits to solemnly proclaim that such an executive order was unlawful and discriminatory. Maneuvering for her fifteen minutes of fame, then Acting Attorney General, Sally Yates, to great fanfare and extensive media coverage, refused to carry out president Trump's lawful order.

Despite her inability to cite any precedent or offer any legal analysis whatsoever for her decision, the Mainstream Media-Democratic Party-Complex immediately elevated the know-nothing Yates to sainthood.

The General Counsel's Office of the Department of Justice, reviewed the order and concluded it was lawful and constitutional. Obama holdover Yates, gave no reasons for her refusal or any factual or legal basis for her contention that the executive order was unconstitutional or unlawful only that she "felt it was unjust."As a card-carrying member of the Resistance, Yates believed her first duty was to serve a higher authority; her role as Acting

Attorney General was secondary. Trump immediately fired this insufferable poseur. Her termination prompted all the predictable media outrage and Yates was depicted as a heroine — a martyr for the cause of the Resistance.

Any impartial first year law student could have seen the politically motivated basis for the federal district court judges decisions in the travel ban cases. Asserting universal jurisdiction over the matter from his federal district court chambers in Hawaii, Judge Derrick Watson pronounced the travel ban unconstitutional on the most dubious grounds. Destined eventually to be overturned by the Supreme Court, he was rebuked for the political basis for his ruling. In the interim, the media championed Watson as a heroic counterweight to the excesses and overt discrimination against Muslims represented by the travel ban.

Shamefully, with the exception of a remarkably sane and level-headed Jonathan Turley, a professor of law at George Washington University, most other alleged legal commentators on the cable TV shows jumped on the impeach-Trump bandwagon. As evidenced by the Supreme Court's ultimate smackdown of the lower court judge, membership in the Resistance for the self-proclaimed legal experts and legal commentators, eviscerated their intellectual faculties, culminating in an inability to separate legal precedent and analysis from their Trump Derangement Syndrome.

The relentless attack against Trump when he issued his travel ban was led by the media who uniformly called his lawful exercise of his presidential power illegitimate. As Turley noted, "For the anti-Trump networks, the legal analysis is tellingly parallel with the political analysis."[7] In the end, all the posturing was for nought as the Supreme Court upheld the ban and the media should have taken the moment to engage in an act of introspection in terms of their outrage and what the highest court in the land ruled. Turley was correct when he observed, "At times the analysis surrounding the immigration order seemed to drop any pretense of objectivity and took on the character of open Trump bashing."[8]

> "Those alleged "legal experts" and other attorneys who should have known better, were swept up in the media maelstrom. Since Trump is a boon for ratings, "hosts and legal experts have shown little interest or patience in the legal arguments supporting his case, even though the Obama administration advanced similar arguments in court."[9]

CHAPTER TWELVE

FBI Spies on Trump Campaign and Mainstream Media Yawns

The Mainstream Media-Democratic Party-Complex continued its role in the Get-Trump movement by acting as a conduit or intermediary for leaks from disgruntled anti-Trump Obama-era holdovers at the Intelligence Agencies. Much of the information was uncorroborated or fabricated, but created the impression that Trump was engaged in unsavory, if not unlawful conduct. The Agencies continued to leak like sieves while the Mueller investigation was ongoing.

Despite the overwhelming and irrefutable evidence of FBI and CIA were conducting unlawful surveillance on the Trump campaign, the mainstream media, once a bulwark against domestic spying by intelligence agencies, suddenly had a change of heart. Reporters transformative moment, miraculously occurred after the election when FBI surveillance on Trump now became unobjectionable, because of the media's predetermination that he was unfit for office. This remarkable indifference regarding the gravity of domestic law enforcement agencies spying on a presidential candidate, was perfectly consistent with the adoption of unprecedented adversarial reporting standards that were farcically justified by the unique danger posed by the new "malignant" presidency.

Nearly every commentator at the major dailies and cable networks refused to call the joint FBI/CIA action an abuse of power.

Had the FBI planted a spy to monitor the Clinton campaign's use of the Steele dossier, what does one suppose the media reaction would be to such a surreptitious and massive abuse of power?

The Democratic Party operated as an agent for undisclosed intelligence agency personnel, as Michael Goodwin noted, "…the Times is so wired into the circle of anti-Trump spooks that it feels qualified to speak for them. So in addition to being the propaganda arm of the Democratic Party, the Times is the flak for crooked cops and spies."[1]

The media also continued to protect their idol, Barack Obama, when he left office even though it became crystal clear that he communicated with Hillary on her rogue private email server. It was clear as well, that Obama participated in the attempt to derail the Trump candidacy through improper use of the intelligence agencies and the FISA court for purely political purposes to facilitate the Hillary's campaign and to preserve his "legacy."

Despite incontrovertible evidence of FBI spying on the Trump campaign, many reporters and pundits incredulously found fault with

Trump for engaging in what they called his illicit war against the intelligence agencies. An example of this distorted perception is found in Natasha Bertrand's article for the *Atlantic* entitled: *The Chilling Effect of Trump's War on the FBI*,

Bertrand, characterized Trump's criticism of the Russia probe in the following manner,

> "The rhetoric, while normal from this president, is norm-shattering. More puzzling, however, is the extent to which Trump has instigated a Republican-led war on intelligence agencies."[2]

Bertrand's article is a bellwether because it is a perfect illustration of Iron Law # 4 for covering the Trump Administration: Deliberately and maliciously, omit to state material facts about a story or report that would make the statements made in the article or report not misleading (legal textbook definition of misrepresentation). Bertrand's article is symptomatic of the complete lack of interest in aspects of the Russian collusion investigation that make it a potential scandal that would far exceed Watergate. Bertrand further described Trump's attacks on the Bureau and the DOJ as unhinged and beyond the pale. Bertrand claimed Trump has,

> " ... raged against the alleged "unmasking" of Trump associates' identities in intelligence reports; the FBI's use of some details in a dossier compiled by a former British spy to bolster its application for a surveillance warrant on Trump campaign adviser Carter Page; and the bureau's use of an informant to monitor members of the campaign with suspected ties to Russia—a tactic Trump has characterized as "spying" and potentially "bigger than Watergate."

The omissions in Bertrand's article are simply astonishing. In one particularly egregious example, Bertrand neglected to mention that the Steele Dossier, upon which the FISA warrant was granted, was paid for by the Clinton Campaign. There is simply no set of facts or journalistic context in which failing to disclose this fact would be viewed as not misleading or the reporter unbiased.

Despite the disgraceful record by CNN of publishing demonstrably false stories on Trump hocked endlessly as "Breaking News", in an article titled, *The Case for a Trump-Russia Conspiracy Is Getting Stronger,* Bertrand nonetheless relied on another one of that network's "bombshell reports." The breathtaking CNN story this time, that former Trump lawyer Michael Cohen claimed that Trump approved a meeting between his son and other unspecified Russians, would later be proven untruthful and added to the growing "Breaking News!"unexploded bombshell reports of CNN. Why would Bertrand continue to rely on information from a network that has turned itself into a laughingstock?

Bertrand didn't entertain the idea that if the Trump Tower meeting was illegal, then the Clinton Dossier was most certainly criminal as well. The fact that this is never discussed by Bertrand with the same vigor with which she devotes to the criminal culpability of the president, is another example of mainstream media reporters acting as extensions of the Democratic Party.

How Bertrand could fail to discuss the likely criminal liability of the Clinton campaign's payment to Steele to dig up dirt on Trump, within the context of the poorly sourced Trump Tower meeting, is simply another staggering omission.

As law professor Jonathan Turley noted,

> "If the Russians had evidence of criminal conduct by Hillary Clinton, her campaign or her family foundation, the Trump campaign had every reason to want to know about it. That is precisely what the Clinton campaign spent millions to do, talking to Russians and other foreigners investigating Trump. Indeed, under this interpretation of federal election laws, Clinton and her surrogates would be equally guilty in using a former foreign spy to gather information on Trump from foreign sources, including Russians.[3]"

In terms of all the media frenzy surrounding the Trump Tower meeting, Turley observed that, "In the end, the Trump Tower controversy is not based on "fake news" as claimed by the president, but the federal crime alleged by the media is based on fake law."[4]

Roger L. Simon accurately described the clandestine connection between the FBI and the Mainstream Media-Democratic Party-Complex, "By providing a willing and virtually unquestioned repository for every anonymous leaker (as long as he or she was on the "right" side) in Washington and beyond, the press has evolved from being part of the solution to being a major part of the problem.[5]"

For the first time in American history, what can only be described as a cabal, tried to interfere in an election and when they failed, did their best to insure that Trump was removed from office or make it nearly impossible for him to govern effectively due to the effect of low approval ratings occasioned by the political media's unrelenting attacks on his legitimacy.

The scandal involved the Obama Administration and members of the Intelligence Agencies working in concert to help assist the candidate of the Democratic Party by spying on the Trump campaign.

This is the type of surreptitious activity that was commonplace in the former Soviet Union. However, while the incontrovertible facts exposed wrongdoing of epic proportions, the media remained silent throughout the burgeoning scandal that involved domestic spying on American citizens through the Intelligence Agencies with the blessing of the Obama Administration.

Where was the Woodward /Bernstein tag team of "deep throat" fame when these monumental abuses of power were unfolding? We know the increasingly witless Bernstein was unavailable due to his almost daily fulminations against Trump on CNN. But Woodward?

Roger Kimball, writing in the *Spectator USA*, does a commendable job in listing many of the facts of the Russian collusion chimera that the media deliberately omitted, because it conflicted or contradicted the Narrative.

The *New York Times* story on how the FBI came to spy on the Trump campaign recalled how George Papadopoulous, during a casual conversation with one Alexander Downer, an Australian diplomat in London, noted that "the Russians" had compromising information about Hillary Clinton.

> "When Wikileaks began releasing emails hacked from the Democratic National Committee in June and July, news of the conversation between Downer and Papadopoulos was communicated to the FBI. Thus, according to the Times, the investigation was born."

> There were, however, a couple of tiny details that the Times omitted. One was that Downer, an avid Clinton supporter, had arranged for a $25 million donation from the Australian government to the Clinton Foundation. Twenty-five million of the crispest, Kemo Sabe. They also neglected say exactly how Papadopoulos met Alexander Downer.[6]"

How ironic, that Trump was mocked mercilessly by the cover-Obama's-backside media when he suggested shortly after his inauguration, that an office in Trump Tower had been bugged, i.e., he was under surveillance. Months later, after the Nunes Memo was disclosed, it appears that Trump may have been on to something and his initial comments, though inartful, may have substantively been correct.

Part Four
Trump Returns Fire

CHAPTER THIRTEEN
The Opposition Party

Any meaningful analysis that seeks the reasons for the hostile interaction between Donald Trump and the political media must begin with an acknowledgement about the nature of the institution arrayed against him. The mainstream media that confronted Trump at every turn, from the latter stages of the presidential election, up to his first day in the Oval Office operates as an extension of the Democratic Party. Trump's attacks against journalists and reporters must be adjudged against this unwavering truth in terms of whether his diatribes and conduct were warranted, or represented, as the media consistently argued, an attack on press freedoms. Reviewing journalists ideological predilections is necessary for an assessment of whether Trump's missives against the Washington media establishment were justified.

"Mainstream Media-Democratic Party-Complex" is an appropriate term to describe the indissoluble nexus between Democrats and political journalists. Others, have used different phrases to denote the relatively new institutional phenomenon. Victor Davis Hanson calls the conglomeration of the entertainment industry, the mainstream media and the Democratic Party as a new "fusion party."

The evidence for such an assertion is bountiful and simply indisputable. When one hears the results of a study conducted by Harvard's Kennedy School Shorenstein Center on Media, Politics and Public Policy, that found the overall coverage of Trump during the first 100 days of his Administration was 93% negative, can any sane individual not agree that such an a stunning and unprecedented finding could never have been recorded had the nation's news media not operated as a de facto extension of the opposition party.

Members of the media are homogenous in their world-view, their education, the social circles in which they travel and their party affiliation. It is a fact that political journalists are overwhelmingly liberal. Every survey that has studied the issue yields the same results.[1]

Journalists over the past twenty-five years have voted overwhelmingly for Democrats by lopsided margins; their views on hot-button issues are consistently liberal and to the left of the country at large. In short, despite their specious protestations to the contrary, there are no conservative employees in the media that could act as a countervailing force to the prevalence of progressive political philosophy to which members of the mainstream media subscribe.

Given this ubiquity in ideological preferences among journalists, it is simply ludicrous to argue that they can put their political preferences aside, like a leopard shedding its spots, and report the news objectively. When the entire journalism profession is comprised almost entirely by registered Democrats, that is exactly the direction in which news is going to be slanted. No other result is or can be possible. Election 2016, was the political event that confirmed this reality.

When there is ideological homogeneity as well as cultural conformity, media bias is not a probability, it is an absolute certainty. Nowhere was this ineluctable fact more apparent than the lopsided pro-Hillary bias during the election.

Prior to the 2016 election, in a moment of pre-Trump uncharacteristic candor, even the *New York Times*, concurred with this assessment of bias, as noted by *Politico,*

> "The people who report, edit, produce and publish news can't help being affected — deeply affected — by the environment around them. Former New York Times public editor Daniel Okrent got at this when he analyzed the decidedly liberal bent of his newspaper's staff in a 2004 column that rewards

> rereading today. The "heart, mind, and habits" of the Times, he wrote, cannot be divorced from the ethos of the cosmopolitan city where it is produced. On such subjects as abortion, gay rights, gun control and environmental regulation, the Times' news reporting is a pretty good reflection of its region's dominant predisposition.[2]"

Thus, as the incontrovertible evidence reveals, the mainstream media Trump faced after the election was an institution that was culturally and politically aligned with the Democratic Party that was determined to exact its revenge, after he had put out to pasture journalists' candidate of choice.

CHAPTER FOURTEEN
Trump Abandons Media's Customs and Rules

Members of the media are an integral part of the political establishment. For Washington journalists, there are unwritten rules and customs to be followed and certain expectations about presidential behavior. In short, political journalists in Washington had every expectation that Trump, like all other presidents before him, would accord them a certain amount of deference. Many acted as if this was their natural right; that it was preordained and could never be revoked by any amount of criticism. Trump jettisoned all these customs on his first day in office.

When Trump unexpectedly won the election, members of the Mainstream Media-Democratic Party-Complex, found themselves in the path of the new president's wrecking ball.

Trump wasted no time in brashly upending the traditional relationship between the president and the press. And, who could blame him? For those who harshly criticized Trump for his pugnacity towards the mainstream media, a question arises: had any other president in recent American history been forced to endure the indignity of being repeatedly compared to Hitler? Once he banished Hillary to the hinterlands, Trump became the object of journalists fury. Barely a week after he won the election, Trump returned the favor by giving the media their first taste of the altered media/White House relationship, when he unceremoniously ditched the press pool to have steak dinner with a friend.

Trump's failure to notify the press corps, was an affront to the political media's delicate sensibilities and enormous self-regard; for

White House journalists, it was a breach of the covenant between president and press — a deliberate breach of protocol. Leaving the press pool in the dark while he dined, was perhaps the first example of Trump's public display of contempt for the media jackals who yearned for his demise.

Based on the hysterical reaction of the press, one might have thought that Tump had ditched the White House press pool while he was en route to a major summit.

The steak dinner incident triggered stern warnings and forebodings from the media about the dangers of a cavalier abandonment of sacred and inviolable media traditions.

Yet for Trump and those within his inner circle, it was an opportune moment to demonstrate how thin-skinned Washington journalists were when it comes to their privileges and perks, which they view as their inalienable right.

A monumental breach of press protocol, intoned a shaken Wolf Blizer, speaking on "The Situation Room."That's unacceptable," he said, "They have got to fix that."[1]

The *Huffington Post* decried Trump's failure to notify the press pool, "The incident continues a pattern of Trump and his team limiting press access and violating basic tenets of press freedom and creates serious concerns about whether he will abide by traditions like holding press briefings and allowing reporters on Air Force One when he is president.[2]"

CNN's Brian Stetler issued the most hypocritical of all the denunciations in terms of the president's failure to adhere to "well-established norms", "While Trump and his aides may delight in irritating journalists, the behavior breaks with well-established norms governing a president's relationship with the press corps Stetler said. Those same norms are also applicable to the president-elect."[3]

Like a pre-teen scuffle between mean girls, the media showed the rest of the country how petty and silly they can be in terms of what constitutes substantive news and what is fluff. In the minds of the American public—which follows the permutations of the journalism business as closely as they follow New Zealand cricket standings", the inside baseball of political journalists is of no consequence.[4]

It was ludicrous to hear the same gang who abandoned "protocol" or "norms" by not affording Trump what every president since Washington had enjoyed — a honeymoon — were now whining, like petulant children, that it was the president-elect who was violating long-standing norms and traditions.

Someone should have alerted journalists to this obvious historical fact. In terms of established protocol, every president since George Washington, including press-nemesis, Richard Nixon, has enjoyed a honeymoon period during which attacks or harsh criticism of the president is held at bay until the chief executive has had time to settle into the Oval Office. However, since the media's preferred candidate, didn't win the presidency, tradition was cast to the wind. So much for adhering to sacred protocols. The hypocrisy of journalists on this score was galling.

Trump's eminently reasonable view was that if the press wanted to be treated with respect to which they felt entitled, they were going to have to practice what they preached and respect the president; courtesy begets courtesy. To the rest of the country this proposition was self-evident; for the purported guardians of our liberties, the idea never crossed their minds.

To add further insult to injury, Trump committed the same breach in "protocols" shortly thereafter when he failed to notify the White House press pool he was leaving to go golfing. Trump's impertinent behavior knocked the media off their exalted perch and put them on notice that he would continue to exhibit the same respect for them as they did for him: i.e., none.

At his press conferences, Trump deliberately refused to call on the usual suspects at this scripted event: CNN, ABC and the major dailies. Instead, Trump called on bloggers and conservative news sites, many of whom were not wire services or affiliated with any major cable networks or newspapers. This clearly got under the skin of the Washington political media establishment.

In addition, after his inauguration, Trump deliberately shut out the prominent players of the Mainstream Media-Democratic Party-Complex, who believed it was their birthright to be granted presidential interviews. The *New York Times* interviewed Trump only four times, NBC News, three times and CBS News and Trump-hating CNN, just once. The mainstream press, ever pious, very much cares about this diminishment in their standing, the plurality of Americans who support Trump and might get him re-elected don't give a shit.[5]

When it came to interacting with the political media in a manner to which they felt entitled, Trump threw the rule book out the window. And who can blame him? All the cries from liberal journalists that Trump was a threat to the freedom of the press were preposterous. The press wasn't "free", they were captive to the Democratic Party and had willingly operated as its propaganda arm for years. Trump wasn't terribly bothered about the wailings of the political media, as they had already declared that it was their moral duty to derail his illegitimate presidency by any means necessary.

CHAPTER FIFTEEN

Trump Attacks the Media as Corrupt, Biased and Out of Touch

Both during and after the election, Trump routinely attacked the media as dishonest, biased and corrupt; a large segment of the population agreed with his assessment. He was right about one thing, journalists are far and away more liberal than the rest of America — a fact that Trump used to his advantage during the campaign as well as during the early days of his Administration.

Trump was not shy about criticizing networks, especially his nemesis, CNN, as well as reporters, whose personal animus towards him continually clouded their judgment as "journalists." Unlike other Republican presidents who preceded him, Trump called a spade a spade. When Andrea Mitchell interviewed Susan Rice, Obama's National Security Advisor, with softball questions concerning her role in improperly using classified information to unmask individuals associated with Trump, he had no compunction whatsoever in quite properly calling her a, "P.R. person" for Hillary Clinton. Trump noted that Rice performed dismally during the interview, "Take a look at what's happening. I mean, first of all her performance was horrible yesterday on television even though she was interviewed by Hillary Clinton's P.R. person, Andrea Mitchell."

Continually exposing such glaring biases only heightened political journalists anti-Trump irascibility. Trump relished calling media reporting "fake news." And, for many stories, breathlessly peddled with increasing frequency, as "Breaking News!!!", Trump's characterization was accurate.

Numerous instances of latent bias abounded, too numerous to recall, but a few notable examples will illustrate the scope of the problem.

Chris Cilliza, now political editor at CNN, repeatedly asserted Trump was sending up smoke screens to hide his legal jeopardy in the Russia Collusion fantasy. Yes, this is the same Chris Cilliza, who as a commentator for *The Washington Post*, during the closing days of the election, instructed us sternly to get off the subject of Hillary's health. On September 11, 2016, shortly after he penned his article, Clinton was caught on video seizing up and passing out as deadweight, appearing to be wracked by rigor mortis and then losing a shoe before being shoved into a waiting van.

Suddenly, for those journalists, like Cilliza who had acted as lapdogs for the Clinton campaign, asking questions about Hillary's health, post-collapse, was no longer grounds for being banished from polite society.

How can anyone ever take Cilliza's reporting and commentary seriously again? When he left the Post for CNN, Cilliza transferred his sterling bias credentials to a new, more appropriate mainstream media venue, where his talents for straining readers credulity would be appreciated.

On the subject of CNN, Mollie Hemingway provided a copious list[1] of instances of journalistic malpractice committed by that network that beggar the imagination. CNN employs reporters and commentators whose glaring conflicts of interest are never disclosed to viewers. These same reporters and commentators have a penchant for deliberately ignoring major stories, such as Susan Rice's unmasking of people close to Trump from intelligence reports. CNN's lack of interest in this truly "bombshell" story was because if investigated, it would be harmful to the Democratic Party as well as former president Obama.

Trump took the occasion during his many rallies, to disparage the mainstream media. He had a sympathetic audience in this regard. And, how could he not be the object of empathy given the repeated instances of outright falsehoods put before the public by his tormentors in the mainstream media. Since his message was carried far and wide during his speeches to supporters, unfiltered by media saboteurs, many journalists, CNN left-wing commentators and reporters, naturally, were keen on repeatedly characterizing these events as frightening "Nuremberg style" rallies, as if the crowd of Trump supporters were all sporting swastika armbands. The trite use of momentous historical events by the mainstream media as part of their anti-Trump crusade, was almost as ridiculous as calling anti-Trump members of the press, the "Resistance", as if harsh criticisms of Trump by journalists were akin to valiant members of the French underground, meeting covertly to plan hit and run attacks on the Nazi occupation forces.

One of the reasons for the political media's preferences for left wing policies and norms is that the nation's capitol is a monotheistic culture. The world of Acelea corridor political journalism is incestuous, as Victor Davis Hanson observed, "Reporters share a number of social connections, marriages, and kin relationships with liberal politicians, making independence nearly culturally impossible."[2]

As bi-coastal elites, Washington political journalists, wear their biases proudly on their sleeves. They harbor the specious belief in their moral and intellectual superiority over their dwindling audiences in the heartland, for whom they have nothing but contempt.

The ideological unanimity, professional and familial interrelationships of Washington political reporters, rife with glaring and undisclosed conflicts of interest, makes a mockery of their ability to be impartial. George Neumayr confirmed this proposition by conducting an examination as unsparing as it is telling. Neumayr's critique is appropriately brutal,

> "It is impossible to overstate the partisan jackassery of CNN, which is at once a product of the cynical, ratings-driven scumbaggery of its head Jeff Zucker and the pretentious liberalism of its "reporters," almost all of whom come from Democratic circles. What an astonishing collection of frauds. With their anchormanish baritones, they try to hoodwink viewers into thinking they are "serious" journalists."[3]

Neumayr notes the connections among journalists at CNN to the Democratic Party are numerous and never disclosed,

> "But they are all just liberal activists playing reporters on TV. Jake Tapper was a Dem staffer. So was Jim Sciutto. Christiane Amanpour, last heard lecturing journalists on the need to drop "neutrality" in its coverage of Trump, is married to former Clinton staffer James Rubin. And the list goes on and on."[4]

In a moment of weakness, even Politico acknowledged the obvious,

> "The "media bubble" trope might feel overused by critics of journalism who want to sneer at reporters who live in Brooklyn or California and don't get the

"real America" of southern Ohio or rural Kansas. But these numbers suggest it's no exaggeration: Not only is the bubble real, but it's more extreme than you might realize. And it's driven by deep industry trends.[5]"

CHAPTER SIXTEEN
The Media's enormous self-regard

In order to eliminate the grandstanding and play acting by some network reporters, most notably, the sanctimonious Jim Acosta of CNN, the White House announced plans to have cameras removed during the daily briefings. Judging by the reaction of the mainstream media, one would have thought that the president had, by executive decree, outlawed the press corps from covering the White House. The delirium occasioned by the proposal reveals the extent of the mainstream media's enormous self-regard as well as their opinion that they are vital for the maintenance of a democracy. For purposes of judging the intensity of the reaction, it is important to note, that Trump merely suggested that the cameras be removed, not that reporters couldn't attend.

In an article ominously entitled, "Democracy Dies in Darkness", *Philadelphia Daily News* columnist, Will Bunch, made the laughable claim that," journalists insistence that the cameras remain will win a lot of newfound respect and plaudits from the American public by standing up for press freedom."[1] Bunch's article is indicative of an enormous disconnect between those issues political journalist consider worthy of note and those issues considered important by the country at large.

The public, which has a dismal view of the media, doesn't care one whit whether cameras are removed from the briefing room. Bunch's frivolous article, reflecting the mindset of the media, was nothing more than an exercise in self-adulation. Members of the media use the cameras as props so they can perform for their fellow peers on a daily basis and applaud one another for how difficult they are making life for the president and as such, performing their sacred duty to speak "truth to power."

No one believes the giddy nonsense expressed in Bunch's article except those journalists who cover the White House. Nonetheless, the camera proposal created convulsions and angst among members of the mainstream media, who flattered themselves that removing the cameras was a grave threat to their inviolable duty, on behalf of a grateful public, to act as fearless bulwarks, against executive abuses of power.

No other incident demonstrates with such salience, the manifest bias, enormous self-regard and devolution into irrelevance of the Fourth Estate than the duel between CNN White House correspondent Jim Acosta and senior Trump aide Stephen Miller at a press conference on August 2, 2017.

Instead of fulfilling his role as a reporter to inform the public by asking relevant and timely questions, the insufferable grandstanding Acosta, a student of the reporter-as advocate-

and-orator school of journalism, engaged in a prolonged debate with Miller about how Trump's proposal to cut legal immigration deviated from traditional American views on immigration. Jonathan S. Tobin of *National Review*, discussed how Acosta's encounter with Miller degenerated into farce,

> "Instead of asking about the issue, Acosta began to grandstand as if he were a member of Congress hogging the camera at a hearing. Acosta asked about the contrast between the text of the Emma Lazarus poem that is on the base of the Statue of Liberty and the proposed bill Trump is backing. That's a loaded question, but hardly unfair. But he didn't just pose the question about the poem or the new requirement that immigrants speak English, or merely follow up when Miller sought to rationalize his position. Acosta interrupted and started debating him."[2]

After viewing the spectacle, a question arises, why is a cable TV "reporter" assigned to cover the White House filibustering at a press briefing? More importantly, as Tobin concludes, "how can he fairly cover this administration in his capacity as a reporter, and not an opinion columnist, if he is using the briefing as a platform for his views on highly divisive political issues?[3]

A comparison of Acosta's play-acting for his peers in the mainstream media with the posture of veteran ABC White House correspondent Sam Donaldson will prove illuminating.

Donaldson was a constant thorn in president Richard Nixon's side during every presidential press conference. As obnoxious and adversarial as Donaldson could be, he never dispensed with or superseded his role as a reporter for that of a partisan advocate. Rather, Donaldson stuck to his script as a reporter, diligently and repeatedly asking Nixon difficult questions, until he was satisfied he had received a meaningful response. The contrast with Acosta couldn't be more pronounced.

Instead of being cashiered for his misconduct, Acosta has remained in his post, constantly whining to a supplicant Wolf Blitzer, about Trump's irascibility while he fights courageously on behalf of the American people.

As the Acosta/Miller incident clearly demonstrated, despite all his character defects, in the eyes of the public, it wasn't Trump, who was the buffoon, it was media clowns like Acosta.

As Tobin reminded us, the cameras in the White House briefing room present correspondents not so much with an opportunity to produce moments of clarity for the public that expose administration failures as it does chances for them to preen in front of their peers and fellow liberals who hate Trump.[4]

CHAPTER SEVENTEEN
Trump Treats the Media With Disdain

When Trump was elected, what drove the media especially rabid was the utter indifference he showed for their collective condemnation of his conduct, the indelicate words he used and his peculiar demeanor and irreverence for Washington rituals and political-speak: Trump didn't give a damn what journalists thought about him or his presidential manners. Since the media had long been accustomed to playing the role of arbiter of good taste and political decorum, dejection by Trump was particularly galling.

Trump accorded the Mainstream media a level of respect consistent with their overt prejudices, dismal approval ratings and ever-eroding lack of trust by the American people.

As Victor Davis Hanson noted,

> Donald Trump has been given a great gift in that his gaffes are seen by most Americans in the context of an obsessed and unhinged Democratic-media nexus. He is pitted against a new fusion party of media elites and aging political functionaries, who all believe that America should operate on their norms, the norms of Washington, New York, Hollywood, and Malibu — all places that symbolize, to most Americans, exactly how the country has gone wrong.[1]

Trump realized what an institution too enthralled with self-regard and self-pity couldn't: Trump's sentiments weren't peculiar, as journalists were despised by a significant portion of the voting public.

Indeed, a Pew survey conducted in May, 2017, found only 21 percent of U.S. adults said national news media are doing a very good job of keeping them informed. The low approval ratings cross party lines: among Republicans, only 11 percent say the news is trustworthy; for Democrats the number is 34 percent.[2] Indeed, according to a national poll, in his the first 100 days in[3] office, more people trusted Trump than the political journalists charged with covering his administration on a daily basis. For the purported guardians of our liberties, the numbers were quite distressing in terms of their ability to mold public opinion. Thirty-seven percent of voters believe the White House has been more forthright than the media, versus 29 percent who favor the press. Another 34 percent were unsure or had no opinion.[4]

Trump also, with ample justification, treated the mainstream media the same way they had treated him: with disdain laced with an animosity that had never before been visited upon a president. Given all the vitriol emanating from journalists and cable TV commentators, could anyone not understand why Trump would respond in kind, given that before he had set foot in the Oval Office, he was the most maligned president in the history of the republic?

Trump not only committed blasphemy by his display of irreverence towards the media's sacred cows, he took his hand, put it on the back of their collective heads and rubbed their faces in it. Additionally, Trump was scorned because he challenged media privilege. The traditional broadcast and cable networks were enraged when Trump deviated immediately from long-established tradition and began calling on conservative or christian news channels during his press conferences. What was especially unnerving to many reporters was that the president dished out as many questions to the media as he received from them.

As George Neumayr of *The American Spectator* noted,

> "Reporters are thrown by a president who questions them as aggressively as they question him. And they resent that he refuses to accept as "facts" what is nothing more than their biased interpretation of the facts."[5]

Vanity Fair's Peter Hanby summarizes this dynamic,

> With the briefing room under his control, Trump and his ill-fated stand-in, **Sean Spicer,** effectively hijacked the network-news cameras, turning them back on the White House press corps, making the once staid question-and-answer sessions into a daily referendum on media bias.[6]

Trump had no compunction mocking reporters who fancied themselves as truth tellers, but were in fact, biased. For those reporters who used the daily briefing press conference as an opportunity to advance their own agendas, Trump treated them as what they were: political hacks. Neumayr recounts an appropriate example where president Trump; contemptuously dismissed a reporter's political-statment-as-question with richly deserved sarcasm,

> "His exchange last week with April Ryan, a correspondent for the American Urban Radio Network, captured that perfectly. She asked him a loaded question not as a neutral reporter but as a water-carrier for the Congressional Black Caucus. So he treated her that way. "I'll tell you what, do you want to set up the meeting?" the president said to her, after she asked if he would meet with the CBC.

> "Do you want to set up the meeting? Are they friends of yours?"[7]

The media wasn't used to a president who challenged them directly and openly questioned their impartiality. Trump expressed his hostility towards the media openly and without apology. As Andrew Malcom noted in *McClatchy*, "Here comes an administration that follows few norms as these creatures of habit and privilege know them. It plays them differently, calls them dishonest and liars. Presidential aides call them the opposition. Shock!"[8]

CHAPTER EIGHTEEN

Trump Knocks Media Off Their High Horse

One of the many examples of the political media's high self-regard was its phony sense of outrage when Trump tweeted a video of his likeness knocking down "fraud news" CNN in a fake wrestling match. Intended as humor, journalists and TV anchors nonetheless were appalled by the video and immediately decried, this brazen display of disrespect as a mortal threat to reporters safety.

While many of the president's supporters online reacted to the video with humor, the consensus among journalists seemed to be that Trump was inciting violence against the media."[1]

Here is a sampling of the over-the-top hysteria occasioned by the video.[2] It is inconceivable, except to those whose sense of self-importance is so misguided, to conclude after viewing the video, that the president of the United States was calling for violence against journalists:

Loyal establishment Republican loudmouth Ana Navarro Tweeted: "It is an incitement to violence. He is going to get somebody killed in the media."

ABC News' chief political analyst Matthew Dowd claimed Trump is "advocating violence against media" and demanded Republican leaders "put country over party" in response to the fake video of fake wrestling.

"Around the world, journalists are murdered with impunity on a regular basis," Poynter managing editor Ben Mullin gravely stated. "This isn't funny."

New York Times reporter Alan Rappeport called the president's tweet "A call for violence against the media."

The Washington Post headlined its news coverage of the tweet, "Trump appears to promote violence against CNN with tweet." WaPo reporter David Nakamura wrote: "A day after defending his use of social media as befitting a 'modern day' president, President Trump appeared to promote violence against CNN in a tweet."

Atlantic editor David Frum similarly took the president's tweet to mean that he was encouraging violence against the media.

New York Magazine writer Frank Rich called the president's tweet "insanity" and "an attempt that might be successful to drum up violence against journalists."

Trump refused to atone for the hilarious video because he knew, that although it was of great consequence for political journalists, it was a non-event for the American people.

Furthermore, the White House understood, as Peter Hanby observed, "that while the media had a high opinion of itself and an even higher opinion of its rebuke-the-president tweets, the public most certainly did not.[3]" Trump's refusal to condemn the video in the harshest terms possible — as demanded by the same people calling for his impeachment — induced conniption fits among sanctimonious reporters.

Mainstream media political reporters were so self-assured in their round-the-clock criticism of the new president, they failed to realize when they were the object of ridicule. When Trump unceremoniously fired James Comey, a media firestorm ensued. Shortly thereafter, Jake Tapper and others who strongly criticized Trump's controversial decision, said sarcastically, the "Russians must be laughing at us right now."

Incapable of even a modicum of introspection, the media truly believed that Trump was the butt of the Russians jokes, when in fact, it was they who were the laughingstock.

Frank Miele, writing in the *Daily Interlake*, provides a lucid explanation as to why the media was the object of ridicule and not Trump,

> "Trump actually got it, and he tweeted Thursday afternoon, "Russia must be laughing up their sleeves watching as the U.S. tears itself apart over a Democrat EXCUSE for losing the election.
>
> "The actual example of that laughter was quite delightful when it wasn't being distorted by the dishonest media. It happened on Wednesday when the Russian foreign minister snorted at NBC reporter Andrea Mitchell for her naivete. Mitchell had shouted out a question to Sergey Lavrov during a photo op with Secretary of State Rex Tillerson: "Does the Comey firing cast a shadow over your talks, gentlemen?" Lavrov first made a joke: "Was he fired?" (as if anyone could have missed that point!) and then he specifically made fun of Mitchell's foolishness to think that U.S.-Soviet relations were going to go on pause because of Comey's employment status. He told her twice, "You are kidding! You are kidding!"[4]

Unsurprisingly, due to their inestimable, self-regard, Mitchell nor any of the other commentators, anchors and reporters got the joke. The reason? Perhaps, as Miele noted, "...

they just take themselves too seriously. Certainly, no one else does."[5]

Despite criticism from journalists who claimed Trump's heavy use of Twitter was "unpresidential", Trump continued to tweet, almost daily. Members of the media seemed to forget that their idol, Obama, used Twitter when he was in office and no one criticized his tweeting as "unpresidential." By way of comparison, here is a question Obama-smitten journalists should have, but never did ask. Which conduct is more "unpresidential?" Trump's excessive tweets, or Obama's taking numerous selfies with the lovely Danish Prime Minister, Helle Thorning-Schmidt, at the funeral service for Nelson Mandela? Was there a journalist in Washington who wrote about this "unpresidential", juvenile and unbecoming behavior?

One of the reasons the media went berserk when Trump used Twitter to communicate was they could no longer filter his message in accordance with their long-established, zealously guarded and cherished role as gatekeepers in terms of which topics or messages will be reported to the public. When he tweeted, Trump not only made the media spectators, he also encroached on what they had always viewed as their domain for setting the political agenda.

Trump's use of Twitter was an effective way for him to deliver his message directly to the America people unfiltered by left wing media lackeys.

For the first time, Trump's unorthodox method of communicating made the media a bit player in the political world of Washington. Journalists thought calling such a novel and unprecedented mode of communication "unpresidential", would force Trump to toe the line and reestablish what the mainstream media viewed as its rightful and traditional role in managing the political conversation.

For Trump's tormentors in the mainstream media, being cut out as the middle man was the ultimate insult — an infraction that would not be tolerated. But, the more they bellowed, the more Trump used Twitter with telling effect.

CHAPTER NINETEEN
Mainstream Media Digs Its Own Grave

For the first six months of his administration, journalists attempted to undermine president Trump by promoting Hillary's pernicious and evidence-free Russian collusion story. Russia, Russia, Russia...If one turned on CNN at any time of day, there would be the same cabal of commentators inveighing against the president and confidently predicting his inevitable demise for stealing the election from Hillary.

Over time, due to their misbegotten zeal, reporters' Trump/Russia stories were based increasingly on "anonymous sources" and in some cases, on only one anonymous source.

Unsurprisingly, mistakes were made, anonymous "sources" lied or were discredited and stories had to be retracted. If the media had any sense of shame, particularly the odious CNN, they would have ceased their "Get-Trump" strategy once their reckless reporting had been exposed as fraudulent and in some cases, defamatory.

For the mainstream media, after the election, shame was a word, that after the election, was rendered inoperative. For members of the Resistance, the concept had no meaning within the context of the Trump presidency.

So uniform was the contempt for Trump among members of the Fourth Estate, that rookie mistakes were made by seasoned reporters who should have known better. An unrepentant CNN had the dubious distinction of setting the gold standard for the dissemination of false stories that shortly after they were breathlessly published and subsequently covered as "Breaking News," were thoroughly discredited.

Mystified as to how Trump's approval rating could possibly be climbing after informing the public for sixteen months about how he was temperamentally unfit for office, Hillary boosters, journalists, CNN anchors and other mouthpieces for the Democratic Party, simply doubled-down on their tiresome anti-Trump rants. How else can one possibly explain "Breaking News" CNN, hosting Stormy Daniels attorney as a guest 58 times in one month? By any standard, such single-mindedness in vilifying Trump, constitutes obsessive behavior.

The media's single-minded pursuit with taking down Trump followed the classic definition of insanity: "doing the same thing over and over again and expecting different results."

Michael Goodwin noted how this fundamental axiom seemed to have escaped the notice of journalists who believed they were a credit to their profession by their feverish attempts to remove Trump from office.

"What started as bias against him has become a cancer that is consuming the best and brightest. In rough biblical justice, media attempts to destroy the president are boomeranging and leaving their reputations in tatters."

He accuses them of publishing fake news, and they respond with such blind hatred that they end up publishing fake news. That'll show him.[1]"

The media's compulsion to rid the country of Trump was nowhere more apparent than in those many instances where journalists' spite for Trump, completely supplanted their sensibilities to follow even the most rudimentary journalistic standards. Media outlets were forced to retract many stories that were proven to be demonstrably false. Given its undisguised loathing of Trump, it should come as no surprise that CNN was one of the worst offenders.

Mollie Hemingway noted the extent of the partiality,

> "CNN's hostility to Trump is off the charts. Harvard Kennedy School's Shorenstein Center on Media, Politics and Public Policy calculated that 93 percent of CNN's coverage of Trump in his first 100 days in office was negative. This media outlet has the most negative coverage of Trump by far.[2]

The unmistakable Get-Trump posture was especially apparent in the commentator panels observed Hemingway. "I recently watched a panel stacked with seven Trump opponents against one Trump supporter. The outlet's leadership reportedly open discusses "war" with the president."[3]

CNN debased itself, yet again, when they were forced to admit that a single anonymous sourced collusion story turned out to be demonstrably false. Members of the Trump hit-squad on the story, authors Thomas Frank, Eric Lichtblau, and Lex Harris, all highly awarded journalists were ignominiously fired. But, they were merely the sacrificial lambs for the network. There were others who made the same mistakes or broadcast "Breaking News" reports that contained misstatements or were highly misleading.

CNN chief political analyst, Gloria Borger, was a fellow offender. Borger and others were part of another get Trump cabal that came on the air with another story, promoted breathlessly with the by-now hackneyed headline, "Breaking News!" The false story was based yet again, on an anonymous source. Borger and other claimed that during his testimony before the Senate Intelligence Committee, former FBI director, James Comey, would contradict Trump's prior assertion that Comey told him repeatedly he wasn't a target of the ongoing Russia collusion investigation. Yet again, the story was based entirely on anonymous sources.

Before Comey's testimony, Borger doubled-down on air, "Comey is going to dispute the president on this point if he's asked about it by senators, and we have to assume that he will be," she said at the time. "He will say he never assured that he was not under investigation, that that would have been improper for him Ethan Sacks to do so."[4]

But Comey's opening statement did support the president's own claim that he had asserted that Trump was not personally under FBI investigation. No one, including Borger was disciplined in any way after the patently false story was peddled, with such bated breath.

"Get-Trump" network CNN, led the way in encouraging reckless reporting. As Mollie Ziegler Hemingway correctly noted, "The serious problems with CNN's approach to the Russia-Trump collusion conspiracy are much deeper than just one story, go back many months, and involve several stories and larger themes that no one at CNN has bothered to sufficiently explain."[5]

As Pulitzer Prize winner Glenn Greenwald, writing for The *Intercept* astutely observed, mistakes made by the mainstream media related to the alleged Trump/Russia collusion story are, "always in the direction of exaggerating the threat and/or inventing incriminating links between" Russia and Trump. Second, that all the false stories "involved evidence-free assertions from anonymous sources that these media outlets uncritically treated as fact."[6]

Time and again CNN put out, under the moniker of "Breaking News", stories that were going to again be the final nail in Trump's coffin, only to make the network and its reporters look like dunderheads as the "explosive" revelations were nothing more than ordinary innocuous events or facts dressed up and presented with breathtaking anticipation. One of the CNN reporters whose fingers were on more than one of the many "explosive" stories that turned out to be duds, was Jim Sciutto, a former Obama Administration employee, whose prior background and affiliation was never disclosed to viewers.

When Susan Rice, Obama's former National Security Advisor was shown to have lied when she said she had no knowledge of any members of the Trump campaign being unmasked. CNN consistently downplayed the story. In addition, as Hemingway observed,

> "CNN's national security correspondent Jim Sciutto, who in addition to being a former member of the Obama administration is also an old colleague of Susan Rice's husband, said, "this appears to be a story largely ginned up, partly as a distraction from this larger investigation."

Host Don Lemon said, "We will not insult your intelligence by pretending otherwise, nor will we aid and abet the people who are trying to misinform you, the American people, by creating a diversion." The chyrons kept claiming the Rice story was "false" even though she herself didn't deny she had unmasked information on U.S. citizens who were political opponents."[7]

As Jason Willick noted in the *American Interest*,

> "if the Fourth Estate is diminished in the Trump era, it will have mostly itself to blame." It deserve blame because it's doing nothing to correct its flaws, it's acting in the same self-aggrandizing manner it has

exhibited for years, and it is showing the same partiality and proclivity to play favorites that it did during the Obama years."[8]

These instances clearly indicated that the media not only had no shame, they had no credibility.

As Lisa Boothe, writing in the *Washington Examiner*, noted at the time, "Trump will also come out on top with his war against the establishment media because they lack credibility. And as CBS' John Dickerson recently said, the 'press did all that good work ruining its reputation on its own.'"[9]

Perhaps the most glaring instance of Trump hatred among journalists was the story published on air by Brian Ross, Chief Investigative reporter for ABC news. Ross claimed falsely that in an "exclusive" report on the Trump Russia Collusion narrative that fired National Security Adviser Michael Flynn would testify that Trump ordered him to initiate contact with unnamed Russians concerning foreign policy while Trump was still a candidate. ABC was forced to retract the story and Ross was put on a four week suspension.

Despite all the media howling about "fake news" being an insult to journalists and a "free press", Ross' egregious and malicious error is yet another instance of reporting on Trump that was patently false and published with the intent to remove him from office. Indeed, Trump was clearly vindicated in his characterization of the report as fake news and the animus against him on which it was based. As he told a crowd in Florida,

> "They took this fraudster from ABC," Trump said. "They suspended him for a month. They should have fired him for what he wrote. He drove the stock market down 350 points in minutes, which by the way, tells you they really like me, right? When you think of it, and you know what he cost people? And I said to everybody get yourself a lawyer and sue ABC News, sue them."[10]

Could anyone claim that Trump's characterization about Ross' story was incorrect?

Since their vanity and self-righteousness precluded them from having any capacity for self-examination, the media ignored the first rule of damage control: when you're in a hole, stop digging. Yet, instead of heeding this rudimentary and self-evident proposition, journalists replaced their shovels with backhoes; with each new castigation of president Trump, they kept digging, sinking further into a credibility morass of their own making.

The mainstream media's post-election collective exercise in self-examination led political journalists to conclude farcically, that their great error during the 2016 election was that they were too hard on Hillary. Yes, the general consensus of those who consorted with Hillary's campaign was that they covered her email chicanery with too much zeal. In this regard, Here is a telling example from Amy "on-Hillary's-speed-dial" Chozick's post-election book, *Chasing Hillary*.

Chozick lamented that poor Hillary had to endure such indignities in terms of the modest coverage about her email machinations. As a *New York Times* reporter from the "paper of record", Chozick couldn't understand all the commotion about Hillary's clandestine private email server. On those occasions when Chozick covered the subject, she was wracked by guilt, writing that her coverage on the issue made her a "*de facto* instrument of Russian intelligence."[11]

In a moment of total incoherence, Chozick asserted on the one hand that she assumed her role during the campaign as a "detached political reporter", yet in the same breath claimed that Hillary's victory party, "was ours."

Writing in *The Federalist*, David Harsanyi put the lack of coverage of the email matter in perspective,

> "The correct way to report on Hillary Clinton is simultaneously treating her like the most competent woman who ever lived but also one who can be easily overwhelmed by emails and simple markings on classified documents. Hillary is not corrupt, her peccadillos are nothing to get too excited about. As

> Harwood puts it, she was "foolish/selfish." Nothing more. Any other framing of Democrats is liable to get the wrong person elected."[12]

How obvious was the media Trump/Russia fixation? Longtime political radical and MIT linguistics professor, Noam Chomsky, had this to say, in an interview with *Democracy Now!*, "Take, say, the huge issue of interference in our pristine elections. Did the Russians interfere in our elections? An issue of overwhelming concern in the media. I mean, in most of the world, that's almost a joke."[13]

When you've lost Noam Chomsky, you've lost the country.

Part Five
Assault On Political Correctness

CHAPTER TWENTY

Trump Assaults the Virus of Political Correctness

For the media, perhaps the most unforgiving of Trump's sins was his broadside attack against the cherished and sacrosanct ideals of the left as embodied in the pernicious ideology of political correctness, that for eight years under Obama had run amok. From the moment he announced his candidacy, Trump tore asunder the speech codes of progressivism and cast them to the wind.

For political journalists, Trump's irreverence for "officially sanctioned" politically correct speech, impermissibly deviated from the norms of conduct expected of Republicans and rigorously enforced by the Democratic Party's communication subsidiary, the mainstream media. Trump deviated from Washington-speak, an artifice that employed euphemisms to avoid conversing about unpleasant truths. For the media, certain terms in the political lexicon were verboten. For example, use of the factually unobjectionable term, "illegal immigrant", to depict those who crossed the border in violation of our laws, was decreed by journalists as indelicate. Since the term "illegal immigrant" was offensive to those immigrants who entered the country illegally, the Narrative demanded it be replaced by the innocuous euphemism "undocumented workers", as if these were people who had inadvertently left their papers for lawful entry into the U.S. on the kitchen table at home prior to their departure for the border.

In order to fully understand the media's frenzy after the election, one must realize that Trump's head-on attack against political correctness was more than a challenge to the language police, it was an assault on the

Washington political establishment, at the apex of which stood the Mainstream Media-Democratic Party-Complex.

When Trump defeated the candidate who was a long-standing member of Washington's political elite, he wasn't assailed so much by the political party he had vanquished, but by an new institution that combined seamlessly the Democratic Party, the major broadcast networks, the entertainment industry and fringe, left-wing academics. This new entity found its ultimate expression and influence during the Obama era. Left-wing academics, the media and the Democratic Party, each had an indispensable role in proselytizing and perpetuating the politically correct Narrative, which has become the philosophical life-blood of liberalism.

Over time, the mainstream media and the Democratic Party had coalesced and become one — the two institutions were indistinguishable. Victor Davis Hanson called the amalgamation a "fusion". Politically purposeless, the Democratic Party had no distinct institutional identity; it no longer provided a,

> "political alternative to conservatism as much as a cultural movement fueled by coastal elites, academics, celebrities — and the media. Its interests are not so much political as cultural. True to its new media identity, the Democratic party is against anything Trump rather than being for something. It seeks to shock and entertain in the fashion of a red-carpet celebrity or MSNBC talking head rather than to legislate or formulate policy as a political party."[1]

Out of this melding between the Democratic Party and the media emerged a new institution — the Mainstream Media-Democratic Party-Complex. This consolidation would eventually debase both institutions.

Frank Miele, writing in the Daily Interlake, described how after the election, when it came time to attacking the new president, the Democratic Party was relegated to playing nothing more than a bit role,

> "Yes, they brought in the usual Democratic hit men to bolster the case that Trump was a danger to

democracy and a menace to the earth, but the Democrats were just supporting actors. The lead role — the Norma Desmond role, if you will — was played by CNN, MSNBC and yes, even Fox.[2]"

Trump's assault on political correctness was more than a long overdue reckoning of one of the most deleterious aspects of liberalism that had crippled the body-politic and stifled free expression, it was also an attack on the corrupt power structure of Washington. Enforcement of the canons of political correctness acted as a vehicle to perpetuate political elites entrenched positions in the Mainstream Media-Democratic Party-Complex hierarchy. Furthermore, political correctness was a way for the elite to assert their moral superiority and force their world-view on the rank and file of the party.

When Trump was elected and failed to temper his forthright manner of speaking nor employ the multitude of euphemism so fancied by the press in an attempt to evade a reality that didn't conform to the Narrative, a hostile media declared war against the new president. The Narrative functioned as the political media's gospel and it was expressed through the vehicle of political correctness. Trump inflamed the media and was considered a heretic because he refused to employ its obfuscatory language in describing reality.

The media accused him of racism; he responded blithely by steadfastly refusing to atone and engage in a futile act of submission. Trump understood any apology offered in good faith would never satisfy the Mainstream Media-Democratic Party-Complex's blood-lust for relentlessly attacking conservatives as racists, white nationalists, etc., etc. — regardless of how they tried to conform to the wishes of the press.

To understand why Trump's election caused such a firestorm within the political media, a review of the state of affairs between previous compliant Republicans and the media will prove instructive.

Prior to Trump's election, the interaction between the media and Republicans never inured to the benefit of the GOP. This is why when Trump was elected, he was reviled by the media because he trashed their wildly successful model for assailing spineless establishment Republicans.

It was dismaying for decades-long loyal GOP voters, to watch the party's leaders cower before the left-leaning mainstream media. For years, the party, especially its consultant class, seemed to relish playing a losing hand: always solicitous of a media elite that despised them, had always despised them and always would despise them.

To view examples of this self-abasement in action, all one had to do was watch, at random, any one of a multitude of cable TV shows to witness the spectacle of the abject Republican guest worked over by the host, who then proceeded unilaterally, to define the political vocabulary and the permissible parameters of discourse on any given topic, with nary a whimper from the enfeebled Republican guest.

A favorite baiting tactic on which party spokesmen would always be ensnared was the subject of protecting or enforcing our borders. Typically, the liberal host would assert that because GOP voters want a secure Southern border, it necessarily followed that Republicans not only hate all immigrants and are racist, but they also are "anti-immigrant."

Few were the instances when the besieged Republican guest would bother to interject and make a distinction between illegal and legal immigration, or bother to expose the linguistic fraud by calling those who broke the law, "undocumented migrants." The Republicans always allowed liberals to define the political vocabulary, unaware of the long-term consequences. Trump was loathed by journalists, because once elected, he promptly ended this charade, long an established and cherished custom of the Mainstream Media-Democratic Party-Complex.

Trump understood all too well how the media played this Get-Republicans-on the-defensive game and how many previous and present Republican politicians inadvertently fell prey to this trap upon which so many were ensnared. Trump was having none of it. Trump infuriated the Washington political media, because he was the first Republican president in recent memory, who refused to oblige the media in this exercise in self-flagellation.

By failing to follow the traditional Mainstream Media-Democratic Party-Complex template of stigmatizing Republicans as racists, Trump became the first anti-postmodernist president. As David Ernst, writing in *The Federalist* shortly after Trump's inauguration noted, "If politics flows downwards from culture, then it was only a matter of time before a politician mastered the role. Love him or hate him, Donald Trump cracked that code.[3]"

Trump played by new rules that he established and that drove Washington journalists right off the edge of the cliff. Trump, unlike so many other establishment Republicans, realized it was pointless to respond to accusations made by partisan journalists. Rather, a new political strategy was required as Ernst noted,

> "If our opponents are going to accuse us of being evil-minded bigots, regardless of what we say or think, then what's the point in bothering to convince them otherwise? Let's play by their own rules of relativism and subjectivity, dismiss their baseless accusations, and hammer them mercilessly where it hurts them the most: their hypocrisy. After all, if there is no virtue greater than authenticity, and no vice worse than phoniness, then the purveyors of contrived PC outrage are distinctively vulnerable."[4]

Trump used progressives strategy against them by avoiding the "Republicans are racists and anti-women" trap. He neither addressed the preposterous, scurrilous and inflammatory allegations leveled against him, nor did he amend his earlier statements that were deemed controversial or beyond the pale because they breached the medias politically correct script from which all Republicans were supposed to read. It was a brilliant act of political deflection and a public display of implicit contempt for his journalistic tormentors.

Instead, Trump simply ignored the charges because as he well knew, "Protesting an accusation from the Left that you're not a racist, sexist, etc. on its own terms is a recipe for failure." As Ernst noted, "Recall what happened to Romney when he desperately tried to demonstrate otherwise with his "binders full of women." Trump dispensed with this pointless groveling and instead, "offered an alternative: rather than make a fact-based, reason-driven argument, let's neutralize the charge by denying its very premises, and in so doing, deny the power of the accuser to render any judgment in the first place."[5]

Because of his audacity in refusing to conform to the media's time-honored rituals, Trump's unorthodox political strategy left the Mainstream Media-Democratic Party-Complex perpetually dazed and confused.

Part Six
Irrelevance of Mainstream Media

CHAPTER TWENTY-ONE
Media is Irredeemably Biased

White House reporting no longer informs the public nor conveys any substantive news. For mainstream media outlets, particularly CNN, their Washington operations have degenerated into a variant of the Jim Acosta show, its audience limited to other White House reporters and CNN anchors.

The mainstream media has become nothing more than an adjunct to the Resistance, a broadcast vehicle whose sole purpose has become to bring down a president who was duly elected. To date, they have been unsuccessful in their quest. In the process, they have tarnished forever, what little of their credibility and standing remained.

Few people watch the rantings of the most virulent cable TV shows. The public stature of the Mainstream Media-Democratic Party-Complex is dismal, approximately half of the country loathes and doesn't trust it to deliver news that is informative and objective and not the product of bias and enmity towards the president.

In short, the political media has reduced itself to irrelevance in terms of where a significant number of people get their news. It will continue its slide into obscurity as Trump continues to occupy the Oval Office and as they persist in their singular purpose of destroying a sitting president.

In the end, it won't be Trump who is defeated, but an institution already in its death throes, that sullied its own reputation by wilfully abandoning all standards for purely partisan purposes. The public understands the mainstream media no longer gathers and reports the news, but rather, merely disseminates the ideology of the Democratic Party.

Political journalists are fond of saying that president Trump has no shame. But as their obsession with the Russia collusion narrative demonstrates, it is the media who has no shame. Its signature accomplishment during the Trump administration is a public audience that continues to decline. Nor does the political media possess the one trait or attribute that could save itself from oblivion: a capacity for self-examination that might lead to rehabilitation with the public.

For the past two years however, there has been no indication that the political media will change course. It will be business as usual, because there is no desire to engage in a mid-course correction. And, this is what will seal the mainstream media's fate — its utter inability to understand why Americans correctly perceive them as nothing more than a wholly-owned subsidiary of the Democratic Party.

Epilogue

As the second year of the Trump presidency approaches, watching the stature and diminished credibility of an unrepentant mainstream media continue to erode, brings to mind Talleyrand's comments about the incorrigible stupidity of the Bourbon dynasty upon their restoration in France, "They had learned nothing and forgotten nothing."

A deranged political media continues with its tiresome and increasingly hackneyed get-Trump message to the exclusion of all other substantive news stories. Political journalists are as inveterately biased as ever and seem to revel in their merging into the Democratic Party to facilitate their solemn duties as members of the Resistance.

The mainstream media furnished indisputable proof of its corruption and allegiance to the Democratic Party, when a cabal of some thirty newspapers, led by the hyper-partisan *Boston Globe*, colluded through their "editorial" pages to protest president Trump's attack on a "free" press. That these leaders of the Mainstream Media-Democratic Party-Complex, had not the slightest idea for how their collective and uniform ideological mindset helped put the final nail in the coffin for the standing of American journalism, indicates the institution is beyond rehabilitation.

Continuing in their role as indentured servants of the Democratic Party, journalists disgraced themselves once more by joining with Democrats in orchestrating a virulent campaign of nakedly partisan attacks against Supreme Court nominee, Judge Brett Kavanaugh. These same Democrats had previously announced before the confirmation hearings had started that they would oppose his nomination to the Supreme Court with every weapon at their disposal, regardless of his eminent qualifications.

When interviewing Democratic Senators on the Committee, no reporters asked partisan and unwavering Democrats on the Committee, why it is they believe 200 years of jurisprudence should be upended and a man with stellar qualifications and character belittled and scorned, because a woman with not a shred of corroborating evidence, claims she was sexually assaulted by Kavanaugh third-six years ago.

The coverage of the Kavanaugh hearings was appalling, both for the ignorance and gross incompetence on display by reporters who let Democratic Senators on the Judiciary Committee make bald allegations and outrageous slurs against an honorable man with no push-back or follow-up questions. This should come as no surprise, for this is the same crop of journalists who covered Hillary's campaign by asking softball or completely inane questions. The episode tells us that a substantial number of reporters have been so indoctrinated in the colleges and universities that they are incapable of intelligently and skeptically interrogating Democratic politicians who revel in their role as demagogues.

Given the disgraceful coverage of the Kavanaugh character assassination by the political media, it is now sadly apparent that the twenty-five year old know-nothings who are slowly infusing the newsrooms, are products of a "higher" education system, that over a twenty-year period has been driven into the ground by liberal and progressive grievance mongering, indoctrination and mandatory reeducation for "privileged" White students.

The Democratic Party today is now entirely captive to the academic dogma of fringe leftists. The manner in which the Kavanaugh hearings were covered is indicative of an institution that is so corrupt and irredeemably biased that it has evolved into a propaganda arm for proselytizing fringe left-wing academic dogma.

The Media's Initial Trump Strategy

[1] Rich Noyes, "Flashback: Journalists Mocked Trump's Announcement as a Joke", NewsBusters, http://www.newsbusters.org/blogs/nb/rich-noyes/2017/01/19/flashback-journalists-mocked-trumps-announcement-joke

[2] Justin Raimondo, "To fight Trump, journalists have dispensed with objectivity", *Los Angeles Times*, August 2, 2016, http://www.latimes.com/opinion/op-ed/la-oe-raimondo-trump-media-bias-20160802-snap-story.html

[3] Ibid

Press Corps: Hillary's Cheerleaders

[1] Larry O' Connor, 8" Minutes Of Shame: Reporters Covering Hillary Embarrass Profession With Softball Questions", *Hot Air*, June 6, 2016, http://www.hotair.com/archives/2016/06/06/8-minutes-of-shame-reporters-covering-hillary-embarrass-profession-with-softball-questions/

[2] "Clinton Email Scandal: How A Biased Press Tried To Ignore It | Stock News & Stock Market Analysis", *Investors Business Daily*, March 28, 2016, http://www.investors.com/politics/editorials/clinton-email-scandal-how-a-biased-press-tried-to-ignore-it/

Trump's Stunning Upset Was a Shock To the Media

[1] Howard Kurtz, "Ugly aftermath: Liberal media types savage Trump, his supporters and the press for upset victory", *Fox News*, November 10, 2016, http://www.foxnews.com/politics/2016/11/10/ugly-aftermath-liberal-media-types-savage-trump-his-supporters-and-press-for-upset-victory.html

[2] Ibid

[3] Leonard Pitts Jr., "Pitts: Maybe we aren't alarmist enough", *Miami Herald*, November 18, 2016, http://www.baltimoresun.com/

news/opinion/oped/bal-pitts-maybe-we-aren-t-alarmist-enough-20161118-story.html

[4] "Trump's Win Is a Reminder of the Incredible, Unbeatable Power of Racism", *Vox*, November 9, 2016, http://www.vox.com/policy-and-politics/2016/11/9/13571676/trump-win-racism-power

Roots of the Media's Psychosis

[1] Brittany M. Hughes, "Trump Won, And The Liberal Media Lost Their Minds", *Media Research Center*, November. 9. 2016, https://www.mrctv.org/author/brittany-m-hughes

[2] Ibid

[3] Posted By Ian Schwartz, "Christiane Amanpour, "Press Faces 'Existential Crisis' Under Trump; 'I Believe In Being Truthful, Not Neutral'", *Real Clear Politics*, November 24, 2016, https://www.realclearpolitics.com/video/2016/11/24/amanpour_press_faces_existential_crisis_under_trump_i_believe_in_being_truthful_not_neutral.html

[4] Jay Caruso, "With One Tweet, Chuck Todd Reveals The Truth About the Mainstream Media", *Red State*, February 17, 2017, http://www.redstate.com/jaycaruso/2017/02/17/one-tweet-chuck-todd-reveals-ignorance-hypocrisy-mainstream-media/

* * *

No Honeymoon For Trump

[1] Richard Cohen,"How to remove Trump from office", *Washington Post*, January 9, 2017, https://www.washingtonpost.com/opinions/how-to-remove-trump-from-office/2017/01/09/e119cc36-d698-11e6-9a36-1d296534b31e_story.html?utm_term=.4004d34ab052

[2] Id

[3] Jazz Shaw,"WaPo writer ponders how to remove Trump from office before he's even sworn in", *Hot Air*, January 10, 2017, https://hotair.com/archives/2017/01/10/wapo-writer-ponders-how-to-remove-trump-from-office-before-hes-even-sworn-in/

[4] As quoted, Benjamin A. Plotinsky, "The Varieties of Liberal Enthusiasm", *City Journal*, Spring, 2010, https://www.city-journal.org/html/varieties-liberal-enthusiasm-13283.htm

[5] Ibid

[6] Ibid

[7] Matthew Continetti, "Trump Short Circuits Washington", *Washington Free Beacon*, February 3, 2017, freebeacon.com/columns/trump-short-circuits-washington/

[8] Rosa Brooks, "3 Ways to Get Rid of President Trump Before 2020", *Foreign Policy*, January 30, 2017, https://foreignpolicy.com/author/rosa-brooks/

[9] Ross Douthat, "The 25th Amendment Solution for Removing Trump", *The New York Times*, May 16, 2017, https://www.nytimes.com/2017/05/16/opinion/25th-amendment-trump.html

* * *

Formation of the Resistance

1. Produced by VinePair Staff / @VinePair, "Chardonnay Helped" Says Clinton Of Election Loss", May 26, 2017, https://vinepair.com/booze-news/hillary-clinton-admits-chardonnay-helped-with-election-loss/

2. Rebecca Traister, "Inside Hillary Clinton's Surreal Post-Election Life", New York Magazine, May 29, 2017, http://nymag.com/daily/intelligencer/2017/05/hillary-clinton-life-after-election.html

3. Ibid

The Russian Collusion Chimera

1. Jonathan Allen & Amy Parnes, "Shattered: Inside Hillary Clinton's Doomed Campaign", (New York: Crown Publishing, 2017), p.394

2. Ibid

3. Ibid, p.395

4. Amie Parnes, "Clinton World dumbfounded by Hillary's election defeat", The Hill, November 10, 2016, http://thehill.com/homenews/campaign/305339-clinton-world-dumbfounded-by-hillarys-election-defeat

5. Ibid, p.395

6. Michael Goodwin, "The media will do anything to bash Trump — and now they're hurting", *New York Post*, June 27, 2017, http://nypost.com/2017/06/27/the-media-will-do-anything-to-bash-trump-and-now-theyre-hurting/

Media Merges Into the Resistance

[1] Victor Davis Hanson, "Our Crude News Network" *American Greatness*, June 6, 2017, https://amgreatness.com/2017/06/06/crude-news-network/

Media Makes Themselves the News

[1] Posted By Ian Schwartz, "Christiane Amanpour, "Press Faces 'Existential Crisis' Under Trump; 'I Believe In Being Truthful, Not Neutral'", *Real Clear Politics*, November 24, 2016, https://www.realclearpolitics.com/video/2016/11/24/amanpour_press_faces_existential_crisis_under_trump_i_believe_in_being_truthful_not_neutral.html

[2] Ibid

[3] Julie Mason, "The White House is at war with reporters, but Trump didn't start it.", *Houston Chronicle*, September 1, 2018, https://www.houstonchronicle.com/opinion/outlook/article/The-White-House-is-at-war-with-reporters-but-13199382.php

[4] Lloyd Grove, "The Journalism Empire Strikes Back", *The Daily Beast*, February 15, 2017, http://www.thedailybeast.com/articles/2017/02/15/the-journalism-empire-strikes-back.html

[5] Varad Mehta, "Journalism's Fake Rebirth: Was It Dead? Maybe Yes", *National Review*, February 22, 2017, http://www.nationalreview.com/article/445129/journalisms-fake-rebirth-was-it-dead-maybe-yes

[6] Ibid

[7] Ibid

[8] Mollie Hemingway, "Media's Refusal To Vet Obama Cuts Credibility On Trump", *The Federalist*, January 22, 2017, http://thefederalist.com/2017/01/22/hemingway-medias-refusal-vet-obama-administration-kills-credibility-trump-administration/

[9] Victor Davis Hanson, "Trump Critics Left & Right Want Him Removed", *National Review*, May 23, 2017, http://

www.nationalreview.com/article/447864/trump-critics-left-right-want-him-removed

A Malignant Presidency

[1] Victor Davis Hanson, "Our Crude News Network" *American Greatness*, June 6, 2017, https://amgreatness.com/2017/06/06/crude-news-network/

[2] Michael Goodwin, "The media's hatred of Trump is only hurting itself", *New York Post*, August 18, 2018, https://nypost.com/2018/08/18/the-medias-hatred-of-trump-is-only-hurting-itself/

[3] Ibid

[4] Ibid

[5] Ibid

[6] Ibid

[7] Jonathan Turley, "Trump's travel ban victory should force media to examine itself", *The Hill,* June 26, 2017, https://thehill.com/blogs/pundits-blog/the-administration/339523-opinion-trumps-travel-ban-victory-should-force-media-tov

[8] Ibid

[9] Ibid

FBI Spies on Trump Campaign and Mainstream Media Yawns

[1] Michael Goodwin, "Defending spies in the Trump

campaign is the height of

liberal hypocrisy", New York *Post*, May 22, 2018, https://nypost.com/2018/05/22/defending-spies-in-the-trump-campaign-is-the-height-of-liberal-hypocrisy/

[2] Natasha Bertrand, "The Chilling Effect of Trump's War on the FBI", *The Atlantic*, May 25, 2018, chilling-effect-of-trumps-war-on-the-fbi/561218/1

[3] Jonathan Turley, "If Trump meeting is illegal, then Clinton dossier is criminal too", *The Hill*, August 6, 2018, http://thehill.com/opinion/judiciary/400609-if-trump-meeting-is-illegal-then-clinton-dossier-is-criminal-too

[4] Ibid

[5] Roger L. Simon,"The Inspector General's Report Will Expose the MSM as Treasonous", *PJ Media*, MAY 18, 2018, https://pjmedia.com/rogerlsimon/the-inspector-generals-report-will-expose-the-msm-as-treasonous/

[6] Roger Kimball, "For your eyes only: A short history of Democrat-spy collusion", *Spectator USA*, May 25, 2018, https://usa.spectator.co.uk/2018/05/for-your-eyes-only-a-short-history-of-democrat-spy-collusion/

The Opposition Party

[1] "The Liberal Media:Every Poll Shows Journalists Are More Liberal than the American Public — And the Public Knows It", *Media Research Center,* https://www.mrc.org/special-reports/liberal-mediaevery-poll-shows-journalists-are-more-liberal-american-public-%E2%80%94-and

[2] Jack Shafer And Tucker Doherty, "The Media Bubble Is Worse Than You Think" *Politico Magazine,* May/June 2017, https://www.politico.com/magazine/story/2017/04/25/media-bubble-real-journalism-jobs-east-coast-215048

* * *

Trump Abandons Media's Customs and Rules

[1] Josiah Ryan, "Wolf Blitzer rebukes Donald Trump", *CNN* November 11, 2016, https://www.cnn.com/2016/11/10/politics/wolf-blitzer-rebukes-trump-for-failure-to-notify-press-of-movements-cnntv/index.html

[2] Marina Fang, "Trump Ditches His Press Pool Again, Violating Media Protocol", *Huffington Post*, November 15, 2016, https://www.huffingtonpost.com/entry/donald-trump-media-access_us_582bc0a1e4b0e39c1fa70613

[3] Brian Stetler, "Donald Trump ditches his press pool again, spurring sharp criticism", *CNN*, November 16, 2016, https://money.cnn.com/2016/11/16/media/donald-trump-press-pool-tension/index.html

[4] Peter Hamby, "How Trump Brought the Political media class to its knees", *Vanity Fair*, November 7, 2017, https://www.vanityfair.com/news/2017/11/how-trump-brought-the-political-media-class-to-its-kneeshttps://www.vanityfair.com/news/2017/11/how-trump-brought-the-political-media-class-to-its-knees

[5] Peter Hamby, "How Trump Brought the Political media class to its knees", *Vanity Fair*, November 7, 2017, https://www.vanityfair.com/news/2017/11/how-trump-brought-the-political-media-class-to-its-kneeshttps://www.vanityfair.com/news/2017/11/how-trump-brought-the-political-media-class-to-its-knees

* * *

Trump Attacks the Media as Corrupt, Biased and Out of Touch

[1] Mollie Hemingway, "Why Is CNN Refuting The Susan Rice Story It Refuses To Cover?", *The Federalist*, April 4, 2017, http://thefederalist.com/2017/04/04/why-is-cnn-refuting-the-susan-rice-story-it-refuses-to-cover/

[2] Victor Davis Hanson, "Presidential Payback for Media Hubris", *Hoover Institution*, March 1, 2017, https://www.hoover.org/research/presidential-payback-media-hubris

[3] George Neumayr, "Trump Is Beating the Media at Its Own Game", *The American Spectator*, February 22, 2017, https://spectator.org/trump-is-beating-the-media-at-its-own-game/

[4] Ibid

[5] Jack Shafer And Tucker Doherty, "The Media Bubble is Real And Worse Than You Think", Politico Magazine, May/June 2017, https://www.politico.com/magazine/story/2017/04/25/media-bubble-real-journalism-jobs-east-coast-215048

The Media's enormous self-regard

[1] Will Bunch, "Democracy dies in darkness, so please turn on the freakin' camera lights!", June 26, 2017, http://www.philly.com/philly/columnists/will_bunch/democracy-dies-in-darkness-so-please-turn-on-the-freakin-camera-lights-20170626.html

[2] Jonathan S. Tobin, "CNN & Jim Acosta – Journalism Harmed", *National Review*, August 4, 2017, http://www.nationalreview.com/article/450152/cnn-jim-acosta-journalism-harmed

[3] Ibid

[4] Jonathan S. Tobin, "CNN & Jim Acosta – Journalism Harmed", *National Review*, August 4, 2017, http://

www.nationalreview.com/article/450152/cnn-jim-acosta-journalism-harmed

Trump Treats the Media With Disdain

[1] Victor Davis Hanson, "Progressive Media & Democrats Form New Anti-trump Party", *National Review*, May 30, 2017, http://www.nationalreview.com/article/448084/progressive-media-democrats-form-new-anti-trump-party

[2] Michael Barthel And Amy Mitchell, "Americans' Attitudes About the News Media Deeply Divided Along Partisan Lines", *Pew Research Center*, May 10, 2017, http://www.journalism.org/2017/05/10/americans-attitudes-about-the-news-media-deeply-divided-along-partisan-lines/

[3] Glenn Greenwald, "The U.S. Media Yesterday Suffered its Most Humiliating Debacle in Ages- Now Refuses All Transparency Over What Happened", *The Intercept*, December 9 2017, theintercept.comtheintercept.com

[4] Gabby Morrongiello, "More voters trust Trump than the political media: poll", *New York Post*, April 28, 2017, https://nypost.com/2017/04/28/more-voters-trust-trump-than-the-political-media-poll/

[5] George Neumayr, "Trump Is Beating the Media at Its Own Game", *The American Spectator*, February 22, 2017, https://spectator.org/trump-is-beating-the-media-at-its-own-game/

[6] Peter Hamby, "How Trump Brought the Political Media Class to Its Knees", *Vanity Fair*, November 7, 2017, https://www.vanityfair.com/news/2017/11/how-trump-brought-the-political-media-class-to-its-kneeshttps://www.vanityfair.com/news/2017/11/how-trump-brought-the-political-media-class-to-its-knees

[7]   Ibid

[8]   "Trump's White House sends arrogant media into Obama withdrawal", Andrew Malcolm, *McClatchy*, January 31, 2017, http://www.mcclatchydc.com/opinion/article129691589.html

Trump Knocks Media Off Their High Horse

[1]   "Media Horrified After Trump Tweets Video Body-Slamming CNN http://dailycaller.com/2017/07/02/media-horrified-after-trump-tweets-video-body-slamming-cnn/

[2]   Ibid

[3]   Ibid

[4]   Frank Miele, "Trump Plays The Outsider Card; Insiders Go Bananas", *Daily Interlake*, May 13, 2017, http://www.dailyinterlake.com/article/20170513/ARTICLE/170519920

[5]   Peter Hamby, "How Trump Brought the Political Media Class to Its Knees", *Vanity Fair*, November 7, 2017, https://www.vanityfair.com/news/2017/11/how-trump-brought-the-political-media-class-to-its-kneeshttps://www.vanityfair.com/news/2017/11/how-trump-brought-the-political-media-class-to-its-knees

Mainstream Media Digs Its Own Grave

[1]   Michael Goodwin, "The media will do anything to bash Trump — and now they're hurting", *New York Post*, June 27, 2017, https://nypost.com/2017/06/27/the-media-will-do-anything-to-bash-trump-and-now-theyre-hurting/

[2]   Mollie Hemingway, "CNN's Latest Retraction Is Just The Tip Of The Fake News Iceberg", *The Federalist*, June 27, 2017, http://thefederalist.com/2017/06/29/cnns-latest-retraction-just-tip-fake-news-iceberg/

[3] Ibid

[4] As quoted, Ethan Sacks, "CNN Forced to Make Correction After Getting Comey-Trump Report Wrong", *The Hill*, https://thehill.com/blogs/blog-briefing-room/336871-cnn-issues-correction-after-comey-statement-contradicts-reporting

[5] Mollie Ziegler Hemingway, "CNN's Latest Retraction Is Just The Tip Of The Fake News Iceberg", *The Federalist,* June 27, 2017, thefederalist.com/2017/06/29/cnns-latest-retraction-just-tip-fake-news-iceberg/

[6] Glenn Greenwald, "The U.S. Media Yesterday Suffered its Most Humiliating Debacle in Ages- Now Refuses All Transparency Over What Happened", *The Intercept*, December 9 2017, https://theintercept.com/2017/12/09/the-u-s-media-yesterday-suffered-its-most-humiliating-debacle-in-ages-now-refuses-all-transparency-over-what-happened/

[7] Ibid

[8] As quoted, Varad Mehta, "Journalism's Fake Renaissance", *National Review,* February 22, 2017, http://www.nationalreview.com/article/445129/journalisms-fake-rebirth-was-it-dead-maybe-yess

[9] As quoted, Lisa Boothe, "Trump exposes the media as partisans", *Washington Examiner*, February 24, 2017, http://www.washingtonexaminer.com/trump-exposes-the-media-as-partisans/article/2615636

[10] Brian Flood,"ABC News' mistake-prone Brian Ross doesn't return from suspension as planned after botching report on Trump, Russia", *Fox News*, January 4, 2018, http://www.foxnews.com/entertainment/2018/01/04/abc-news-mistake-prone-brian-ross-doesn-t-return-from-suspension-as-planned-after-botching-report-on-trump-russia.html

[11] As quoted, David Begley, "David Begley: The Frozen Chozick",

Power Line, April 27, 2018 https://www.powerlineblog.com/archives/2018/04/david-begley-the-frozen-chozick.php

[12] David Harsanyi, "After Self-Reflection, Journalists Discover They've Been Too Critical Of … Democrats", *The Federalist*, September 19, 2017, http://thefederalist.com/2017/09/19/after-serious-self-reflection-journalists-discover-theyve-been-too-critical-of-democrats/

[13] Tim Hains, "Noam Chomsky: In Most Of The World, Media Obsession With Trump-Russia Interference Story Is 'A Joke'", *Real Clear Politics*, August 20, 2018, https://www.realclearpolitics.com/video/2018/08/20/noam_chomsky_in_most_of_the_world__trump-russia_collusion_story_is_sen_as_a_joke_media_ingnores_serious_issues.html

Trump Assaults the Virus of Political Correctness

[1] Victor Davis Hanson, "Progressive Media & Democrats Form New Anti-Trump Party", National Review, May 30, http://www.nationalreview.com/article/448084/progressive-media-democrats-form-new-anti-trump-party

[2] Frank Miele, Trump plays the outsider card; insiders go bananas, *The Daily Interlake*, May 13, 2017, http://www.dailyinterlake.com/opinion/column/frank-miele

[3] David Ernst, "Donald Trump Is The First President To Turn Postmodernism Against Itself", *The Federalist*, January 23, 2017, http://thefederalist.com/2017/01/23/donald-trump-first-president-turn-postmodernism/

[4] Ibid

[5] Ibid

Made in the USA
Monee, IL
15 November 2020